See What We Say

See What We Say

Situational Vocabulary for Adults Who Use Augmentative and Alternative Communication

by

Barbara Collier

Baltimore • London • Toronto • Sydney

Paul H. Brookes Publishing Co.
Post Office Box 10624
Baltimore, Maryland 21285-0624

www.brookespublishing.com

Typeset by Eastern Composition, Binghamton, New York.
Manufactured in the United States of America by
Versa Press, East Peoria, Illinois.

The creation of the original version of this manual was supported by Harmony Place Support Services, The Gage Transition to Independent Living, and Participation Apartments–Metro Toronto through a grant from The Ontario Trillium Foundation, Canada. Subsequent support was provided by Harmony Place Support Services, Toronto, Canada.

All examples in this book are composites. Any similarity to actual individuals or circumstances is coincidental, and no implications should be inferred.

A portion of the proceeds from the sale of this book goes to Harmony Place Support Services, an employment and education program for adults who use augmentative and alternative communication.

Library of Congress Cataloging-in-Publication Data

Collier, Barbara
See what we say: situational vocabulary for adults who use augmentative and alternative communication / by Barbara Collier.
p. cm.
Includes bibliographical references.
ISBN 1-55766-469-2
1. Handicapped—Means of communication. 2. Communication devices for the disabled. I. Title.

RC423.C59 2000
616.85'503—dc21 00-036023

British Library Cataloguing in Publication data are available from the British Library.

In loving memory of my father,
Kevin A. Collier

Contents

About the Author

Barbara Collier has worked in the augmentative and alternative communication (AAC) field as a speech-language pathologist with The Pediatric Augmentative Communication Service at The Bloorview MacMillan Centre (formerly The Hugh MacMillan Rehabilitation Centre) in Toronto, Canada, and as Director of The Adult Adaptive Communication Service. In 1997, she was Senior Consultant of AAC Service Development and Training with The Ontario Ministry of Health's Assistive Devices Program, Toronto, Canada. She currently is an independent consultant in Toronto, where she provides communication training programs for AAC users, family members, and community agencies.

Barbara has presented many papers, courses, and workshops on AAC. She is an invited speaker at national and international conferences and is the recipient of a number of awards for her work in the field. She is also the writer, director, and producer of the videotape *Communicating Matters: A Training Guide for Personal Attendants Working with Consumers Who Have Enhanced Communication Needs* (available with accompanying guidebook from Paul H. Brookes Publishing Co., 2000).

Foreword

A number of years ago, I met a young woman named Mary. She had cerebral palsy and used an old communication board containing several photographs of family and other people, some pictures of favorite foods, and the word *toilet*. Reports indicated that Mary was very passive and not motivated to communicate. When we first met, Mary held her head down and showed little interest in interacting with me. After a few unsuccessful attempts to interact, I brought out an array of line drawings and words. Mary's eyes suddenly lit up. We spent several hours reviewing items; she indicated which ones she wanted on her new communication display. Within a few hours, Mary was telling me about her family, her love of animals and music, her concerns about her current living situation in a nursing home, and her dreams for the future. Think about it: Here was a young woman with so much to communicate and share with others, yet all she was able to communicate for many years were the names of some family members and other people, or requests for a few favorite foods or to go to the bathroom. Mary had an augmentative and alternative communication (AAC) system, but it was a miserable failure because it did not provide her with a way to meet her most important communication goals. It failed because it did not give Mary access to appropriate vocabulary.

People are only able to attain their communication goals and realize their full potential if they have effective means to convey their thoughts, feelings, and ideas to others. Many children and adults such as Mary have significant communication disabilities that preclude them from relying on natural speech to communicate with others. The advent of AAC systems (e.g., signs, communication books with line drawings, alphabet boards, computer-based technologies with voice output capabilities) has offered these individuals the potential for increased communication. Nevertheless, AAC systems only enhance communication *if* they incorporate appropriate vocabulary that allows the individual to attain his or her goals. In fact, according to Carlson (1981), when an AAC system is not effective, it is usually because the vocabulary included in the system is not appropriate. This was certainly true in Mary's case.

At first glance, the task of selecting appropriate vocabulary appears to be easy—just choose the words that the individual needs to communicate. In practice, however, it is one of the most (if not *the* most) challenging tasks in implementing effective AAC systems. If vocabulary is to be effective, it must

- Allow the individual to meet his or her unique communication needs within daily life
- Be appropriate to the individual's age, gender, and cognitive and linguistic skills
- Be appropriate to the individual's cultural and family background
- Be unique to the individual, reflecting his or her personality, interests, and priorities

In addition, vocabulary must be reviewed and updated regularly to accommodate changes in the individual's needs and skills.

A number of approaches to vocabulary selection have been proposed in the AAC field. These include techniques such as

- Brainstorming with the AAC user and his or her communication partners (Morrow, Mirenda, Beukelman, & Yorkston, 1993)
- Completing ecological inventories (i.e., observations of the individual and peers in typical environments to determine communication needs and specific vocabulary needs) (Sigafoos & York, 1991)
- Reviewing word lists (i.e., lists of words derived from natural speakers or individuals who require AAC) (e.g., Beukelman & Mirenda, 1998; Yorkston, Beukelman, Smith, & Tice, 1990; Yorkston, Dowden, Honsinger, Marriner, & Smith, 1988)
- Completing communication diaries (i.e., notebooks used to track and record communication breakdowns and vocabulary needs) (Yorkston, Honsinger, Dowden, & Marriner, 1989)

At the beginning of the 21st century, however, few tools are available to support individuals who use AAC, their families and friends, and professionals in the challenging process of selecting appropriate vocabulary. No vocabulary selection technique discussed in the literature is sufficient in and of itself for selecting appropriate vocabulary for an individual. A clinician can use multiple techniques to increase the breadth of vocabulary selected, but this approach results in significant redundancy of vocabulary selected across the different techniques. Using multiple techniques also requires a significant investment of time from the informants—family, friends, and professionals who may already be overextended with other caregiving demands.

In *See What We Say: Situational Vocabulary for Adults Who Use Augmentative and Alternative Communication,* Barbara Collier provides a comprehensive selection tool to support adults who use AAC, their families and friends, and professionals in meeting daily vocabulary needs. This tool offers a highly effective and efficient approach to vocabulary selection for adults who require AAC. *See What We Say* provides the following:

- Step-by-step procedures for selecting and updating vocabulary that is truly responsive to the individual's unique needs
- Vocabulary suggestions to address a variety of important communication needs (e.g., directing personal services, interviewing service providers, using the telephone, eating out, social conversations)

See What We Say is particularly unique because it is written not only for speech-language pathologists and other professionals, but also for adults who use AAC and their families and friends. Significant input regarding the development of the book came from adults who use AAC; they were instrumental in identifying communication topics and contexts for inclusion. Through this book, Barbara Collier provides the AAC field with an important tool to ensure that adults who use AAC, such as Mary, have access to the vocabulary that they need to meet their goals and achieve their full potential.

Janice C. Light, Ph.D.
Department of Communication Disorders
Pennsylvania State University

REFERENCES

Beukelman, D.R., & Mirenda, P. (1998). *Augmentative and alternative communication: Management of severe communication disorders in children and adults* (2nd ed.). Baltimore: Paul H. Brookes Publishing Co.

Carlson, F. (1981). A format for selecting vocabulary for the nonspeaking child. *Language, Speech and Hearing Services in Schools, 12,* 140–145.

Morrow, D., Mirenda, P., Beukelman, D., & Yorkston, K. (1993). Vocabulary selection for augmentative communication systems: A comparison of three techniques. *American Journal of Speech Language Pathology, 2,* 19–30.

Sigafoos, J., & York, J. (1991). Using ecological inventories to promote functional communication. In J. Reichle, J. York, & J. Sigafoos (Eds.), *Implementing augmentative and alternative communication: Strategies for learners with severe disabilities* (pp. 61–70). Baltimore: Paul H. Brookes Publishing Co.

Yorkston, K., Beukelman, D., Smith, K., & Tice, R. (1990). Extended communication samples of augmented communicators: II. Analysis of multi-word sequences. *Journal of Speech and Hearing Disorders, 55,* 225–230.

Yorkston, K., Dowden, P., Honsinger, M., Marriner, N., & Smith, K. (1988). A comparison of standard and user vocabulary lists. *Augmentative and Alternative Communication, 4,* 189–210.

Yorkston, K., Honsinger, M., Dowden, P., & Marriner, N. (1989). Vocabulary selection: A case report. *Augmentative and Alternative Communication, 5,* 101–108.

Preface

People who use augmentative and alternative communication (AAC) and cannot independently spell out what they want to communicate must rely on someone else to assist them in selecting vocabulary. Many AAC users say that the words they need are often not available to them on their displays or devices.

In 1996–1997, I spent some time discussing this dilemma with 13 adults who use AAC and soon realized that we had much to learn from each other. Some AAC users had excellent vocabulary and tips for certain situations, and they were only too willing to share their insights with others. Nonetheless, most of the AAC users in this group did not have the vocabulary they needed to communicate, and they participated in selecting the situations and vocabulary shared here.

See What We Say: Situational Vocabulary for Adults Who Use Augmentative and Alternative Communication is a compilation of vocabulary and tips provided by AAC users, speaking people with disabilities, and service providers. This book is addressed directly to AAC users and their team members. I hope that both AAC users and service providers will use the book in whatever manner they find helpful. For some, it may serve to help select words and phrases; for others, it may be a resource for tips about communicating in certain situations.

This book is by no means a definitive list of vocabulary. It is not based on any formal research and merely proposes suggestions for certain situations. My intent is for *See What We Say* to be used as a resource for selecting vocabulary. It should not, however, be the only resource. Readers are encouraged to check the resources provided in the References and Vocabulary Resources section and to work closely with their AAC clinicians to determine additional vocabulary.

Acknowledgments

I would like to thank Harmony Place Support Services, The Gage Transition to Independent Living, and Participation Apartments–Metro Toronto, who were supported in the creation of the original version of this manual by a grant from The Ontario Trillium Foundation, Canada. Subsequent to the development of the original manual, Harmony Place Support Services, under the leadership of Nancy Haans, continued to provide support. Without their assistance and Nancy's belief in the project, this manual never could have been completed.

There are many people who must be recognized for their input and contributions to this manual. They include AAC users, family members, friends of AAC users, and service providers. I am indebted to Joe Arnold, Carol Berube, Mark Campbell, Marsha Cook, Laura Forma, Darlene Gallant, Sarah Griffiths, Tami Hawes, Joe Jessop, Kim Knox, Laura Lisker, Michael Millard, Lynnette Norris, Cathy O'Connell, Sherri Parkins, Anne Marie Renzoni, Bruce Rubinstein, Ann Running, Marcello Santos, Aaron Shelbourne, Don Smith, Tracey Swift, Gail Teachman, Chris Webley, and Jesse Zone. I would like to extend a special thanks to Donna Castanheiro and Paul Janzen for their technical and clerical assistance on early versions.

I am especially grateful to my family, friends, and colleagues who supported me throughout the project. In particular, I would like to thank Susie Blackstein-Adler, Melanie Fried-Oken, Anne Warrick, Joan Monahan, Ruth Collier, and Bill Bobek for their encouragement and support.

It has been a pleasure working with and learning from the team at Paul H. Brookes Publishing Co. I will almost miss the daily e-mails from Elaine, Nicole, Lisa, Erin, and Amy.

A very special thanks to Janice C. Light. She has captured the essence of what this book is about in her foreword. Like so many people in the field of AAC, I value Janice's insight and wisdom. She has inspired my work for years, and I am truly grateful for her generosity and her willingness to share her ideas and for encouraging me to bring this manual to a wider audience.

Prologue

Some people have difficulty speaking due to disabilities such as cerebral palsy, traumatic brain injury, developmental delay, and autism. Having a severe speech problem influences many aspects of a person's life. It may affect his or her ability to live in the community, to direct his or her care, to find employment, and to make and keep friends. These situations can be greatly improved, however, with augmentative and alternative communication.

WHAT IS AUGMENTATIVE AND ALTERNATIVE COMMUNICATION, AND WHO USES IT?

Augmentative and alternative communication (AAC) refers to ways other than speech that are used to communicate. AAC users typically utilize a number of aided and unaided communication systems based on their needs and skills. *Aided AAC systems* might include communication displays, which are composed of written words, letters or phrases, or pictures or symbols; devices that speak or print out messages; and call bells. Specialized AAC services are available to assist people in determining the AAC systems that best meet their needs and skills. *Unaided AAC systems,* which do not require an external aid, might include voice, speech, nodding and shaking one's head, facial expression, pointing or looking at desired objects, gestures, and sign language. Most AAC users employ a variety of these unaided communication methods.

WHY DO USERS OF AUGMENTATIVE AND ALTERNATIVE COMMUNICATION NEED VOCABULARY?

AAC users who cannot point to letters of the alphabet to spell out the words they need can often use pictures, whole printed words, or symbols to communicate. With the exception of some newer models, most AAC devices require someone other than the user to add these pictures and symbols to the display or device. As a result, AAC users often find that they do not have the vocabulary they need in order to communicate. It is hoped that *See What We Say: Situational Vocabulary for Adults Who Use Augmentative and Alternative Communication* will provide some suggestions for words you might want included on your display or in your device.

WHO MIGHT BENEFIT FROM THIS BOOK?

See What We Say is intended for people who have AAC systems in place, live in a community environment, and want to participate in community activities. This book may assist them—as well as their families, clinicians, life skills workers, and support service providers—in selecting words and phrases they might need to communicate in these environments. The vocabulary is presented in the form of printed words. AAC users who use pictures or symbols will need to have the words they want represented either in pictures or symbols. Corresponding graphics are not presented in this book because the individual AAC user should be involved in selecting the graphics that represent his or her vocabulary.

Two groups of AAC users could potentially benefit from this book:

1. People who use pictures or symbols to communicate because they have problems spelling words
2. People who spell but find it faster and easier to use whole words or phrases in addition to spelling

See What We Say is not intended for people who are just starting to communicate. If a person does not have a communication system in place, he or she should contact an AAC service. Clinicians with special training in AAC will assist him or her in finding the best ways to communicate.

HOW WERE THE SITUATIONS AND VOCABULARY SELECTED FOR THIS BOOK?

Thirteen AAC users who live in the community were interviewed. They suggested situations in which they felt they needed to communicate more effectively. The situations that were common to most of these AAC users are presented in this book. Other environments are not discussed in *See What We Say* because excellent resources for many of them already exist (e.g., communicating in a workshop environment, communicating when playing a game of cards). Such resources are found in the References and Vocabulary Resources section of this book.

The words and phrases used for the situations addressed in *See What We Say* have been collected from AAC users, family members, educators, support service providers, and AAC clinicians. In some cases (e.g., directing one's services), vocabulary was collected by listening to what speaking people with disabilities said in similar situations. For advocacy and sexuality, vocabulary was based on existing literature and research. For other topics of high interest to AAC users, words and phrases were selected from articles and books on the subject. The result is a collection of words and phrases, and it is up to you to choose the ones you want.

HOW WERE THE TIPS AND RESOURCES COLLECTED?

In addition to suggested vocabulary, *See What We Say* contains some tips and resources that may be helpful for AAC users. Please note that these tips are suggestions only. What works for one AAC user may not work for you.

Introduction

Updating Your Vocabulary

Some augmentative and alternative communication (AAC) users like to update their vocabularies extensively every year. Other AAC users update their vocabularies when there is a significant change in their lifestyle (e.g., moving into an apartment, beginning to direct one's own services). There is still a need, however, for regular updating of one's vocabulary. Most of the AAC users who contributed to this book report that, ideally, they need at least 30–45 minutes every 2 weeks to maintain their display or device vocabularies. There are a number of steps you might want to consider when updating your vocabulary.

FINDING AN ASSISTANT IF YOU NEED ONE

Some individuals who use voice output devices may choose to go through the book on their own and program the words they want into their devices or computers. Other AAC users may need an assistant (e.g., family member, friend, service provider, clinician) to help read through this book and add the words that the AAC user wants incorporated in his or her device or display. If so, plan on booking sufficient time for this endeavor or it will be frustrating. You will be surprised how many tangents you will take, as many of the topics and tips are interesting and deserve to be discussed.

DETERMINING THE TYPE OF VOCABULARY YOU NEED

To assist you in deciding what words you need to communicate, it may be useful to consider three categories of vocabulary:

- Personal vocabulary
- Frequently used or core vocabulary
- Situational vocabulary

Personal Vocabulary

Your personal vocabulary includes the specific names of people about whom you communicate (e.g., *Jane, Mrs. Brown*), the places you go (e.g., *grocery store, pharmacy*), and words about your hobbies and interests. Appendix A lists headings that might help you in developing your personal vocabulary. Remember to review this list regularly to add necessary words and to delete ones that you no longer use or need.

Frequently Used or Core Vocabulary

In addition to personal vocabulary, you may need frequently used phrases (e.g., *How are you? I'm fine, thanks, I'd like . . .*) or phrases that must be communicated quickly (e.g., *I need some help*). You may also need single words that can be combined to make sentences, such as the pronouns *I, you, he,* and *she* and the verbs *am, are, was,* and *have.* The number of frequently used words—often referred to as *core vocabulary*—tends to be small. These words are usually organized in ways that support sentence production. For instance, words or pictures are arranged into groups, such as action words, descriptors, questions, and nouns. Because they are used so often, it is best to keep these words in an easily accessible place (e.g., on the tray of a wheelchair, in the first few pages of a communication display folder, on the first overlay of a communication device). See References and Vocabulary Resources at the end of the book for more information about frequently used words for sentences.

Situational Vocabulary

Situational vocabulary is often called *fringe* or *context* vocabulary. It refers to the words used in certain situations. For example, one uses words about money when in a bank, words about food when ordering at a restaurant, and words about locations and time when booking transportation. AAC users who use displays often keep situational vocabulary on separate pages in a binder or folder or in an appropriate place (e.g., vocabulary about dressing and grooming is kept in the bedroom). Some AAC users take their entire binders or folders with them in a carry bag on the back of their wheelchairs, and others choose to take the specific pages they require for that day. Situational vocabulary, typically utilized along with one's frequently used and personal vocabularies, is the type of vocabulary included in this book.

SELECTING THE SITUATIONS IN WHICH YOU NEED TO COMMUNICATE

You can use the Table of Contents to identify which situations are important to you. Even if you are not currently participating in a certain situation or activity (e.g., maintaining your wheelchair), you may want to consider reviewing its vocabulary. Sometimes AAC users are not involved in a particular activity simply because they do not have the vocabulary or the opportunity. This is a good time to make changes! Think of other such situations that are not included in this book, and plan on selecting vocabulary for these situations.

SELECTING THE VOCABULARY

You do not need every word and phrase presented in this book. They are only suggestions and should be used as a starting point. In fact, having too many words might cause trouble when you have to find the one specific word you have in mind. This will slow you down when you are having a conversation. It is better to select a few appropriate words and phrases and use them well than to have too many and not know where to find them.

It is suggested that you use the vocabulary listed in this manual to inspire you to think of other words that may be more pertinent to you. Yet do not limit yourself to choosing your vocabulary only from the lists presented in this manual. There are many other useful techniques for selecting vocabulary. Some include recording the words and phrases of people who speak in similar situations, inviting people who know you well to suggest words and phrases that they think you might need to communicate, and checking out researched vocabulary lists that match your age and gender. Most AAC users employ a combination of these approaches.

It is important that you are involved in all aspects of selecting and organizing your vocabulary. If someone else does it for you, you may not agree with his or her choice of words. It is also likely that you will have greater problems locating the words in your display or device. This manual's vocabulary lists contain two columns to help you consider each word and keep track of the words and phrases you want. These two columns are further described in the following sections.

Add (Column 1)

This column indicates items that you want added to your display or device. You or your assistant can put a checkmark beside the appropriate words or phrases. It is recommended that you listen to all of the suggested vocabulary first and then go back over each item one by one.

Something Like This (Column 2)

Placing a checkmark in this column means you like the idea but want to communicate it differently. For example, you might place a checkmark in the "Something like this" column next to the message *What's my balance?* It could then be rephrased as *I'd like to know how much is in my bank account.* Customize the words and phrases to reflect how you might communicate that idea. Take your age, culture, and personality into consideration. Remember that you can use slang or contemporary phrases and sayings to communicate your ideas as well.

Placing a check in this column can also mean that you want something similar to the word just mentioned. For example, you want the word *neckrest* and the closest word you have heard is *headrest.* If you tell your communication partner you want "something like this" after hearing *headrest,* it will help him or her suggest similar words, such as *neckrest.* When your partner guesses what you want, he or she can write the word in this column.

REPRESENTING YOUR VOCABULARY

There are three important steps to follow when determining how to represent your vocabulary. First, decide if an item you want should be represented by a word or a phrase. Second, make sure that the words you want are represented in a way you can recognize (e.g., print, photographs, symbols). Third, organize your vocabulary so you can easily find the words you want. These three steps are discussed in detail next.

Decide Whether You Need a Word or a Phrase

You need to decide whether you want a word to appear on its own or as part of a phrase or sentence. For instance, if your vocabulary only shows the word *wheelchair* as part of the sentence *Please charge my wheelchair battery,* you will not be able to use *wheelchair* in any other way. It will be stuck in that sentence. Nonetheless, you will want frequently used phrases incorporated in your vocabulary so you do not have to take the time to construct these sentences every time you want to communicate them. There are no rules for determining whether words appear individually or in phrases; you will have to use your own judgment. Some guidelines to assist you in this decision-making process follow.

Choose a single word if

- You need to use it in different sentences

Choose a phrase if

- You use that phrase regularly
- It is a frequent sentence starter (e.g., *I want, I'd like to, I wonder if, Would you*)
- You need to convey the information in a hurry (e.g., a request for help)
- The message is long and requires too much time and effort to construct word by word or letter by letter

Represent Your Vocabulary in a Way that Makes Sense to You

If you use printed words and phrases to communicate, your vocabulary should be printed in words and phrases. The words and phrases can be clearly handwritten or typed into and printed from a computer. Some AAC users like to have their words appear in either upper- or lowercase letters, and some find it difficult to read others' cursive handwriting. Have your assistant develop a few samples of different styles so you can choose the one that you prefer. If you have a computer, you can also experiment with different fonts and sizes. In addition, some AAC users find it easier to see the words and phrases if they appear in black print on colored backgrounds (e.g., yellow, light blue).

Some picture-based AAC devices are equipped with their own set of pictures; others allow you to pick the type of picture you want. If you use pictures to communicate and your system allows you to choose the pictures, your vocabulary should be represented using the type of pictures you prefer. There are many good resources for pictures. For example, there are stamp books and computer software programs that can be used to make displays and overlays. By utilizing these software programs, you or your assistant can easily change the content, size, color, and arrangement of your displays. (Contact your AAC clinician or speech-language pathologist for more information.) Remember that you can always mix and match different styles of pictures (e.g., photographs, line drawings, colored pictures). Just make sure that you choose the pictures (not someone else), that they make sense to you, and that you can remember the words or phrases they represent. In addition, always have the word or phrase typed or printed above, below, or beside the picture or symbol. That way your partner knows what you mean when you point to that particular picture on a display.

Blissymbols and other symbol-based systems can represent what you want to communicate on displays and many AAC devices. Thus, if you use this system to communicate, you may want your new vocabulary to be represented in Blissymbols. As with picture systems, software programs and stamp books are available to assist people in making Blissymbol displays. People who use Blissymbols learn the meaning of these symbols and the concepts they represent. It is important that Blissymbol users are supported in their learning of the system. AAC users and tutors can get more information on Blissymbols from their AAC service provider or speech-language pathologist or from Blissymbolics Communication International (see Appendix B for address).

Organize Your Vocabulary

Organize your vocabulary so that you know where to find words and phrases. Most AAC users like to arrange their vocabulary in ways that make sense to them. For example, John has a page in his device with his transportation words, another for grocery shopping, and another for participating at his conferences. Susan keeps her routine service instructions on a corkboard beside her bed. Jean has her frequently used vocabulary on the tray of her wheelchair and additional vocabulary arranged in a binder. Each day she chooses the pages she needs, depending on what she has planned for the day.

If your system already has a specific organization (e.g., foods in one place, time words in another)—and if this arrangement suits your needs—you can continue to use it by adding new pages or overlays. It is a good idea to add tabs (available at most stationary stores) to the tops or sides of your pages. These are like bookmarks that stick out from the pages. Words or pictures can appear on the tabs. For example, a picture of a car or bus could mark your page of transportation words. Tabs also help some AAC users turn the pages. People who use their eyes to communicate can look at them to indicate the page to which they want their partners to turn.

AAC users whose devices involve codes or overlays to retrieve their programmed words should follow the organizational setup and rules that they already use. If you require aid in this matter, you should contact the clinician or vendor who assisted you in selecting your device and follow the instructions for programming your specific device.

PRACTICING USING YOUR NEW VOCABULARY

Although having the words and phrases you need for a certain situation is essential, you also need to have the skills to communicate in that environment. This involves knowing how to operate your device or to find words on your display, how to communicate with different partners, which communication technique to use (e.g., your device, gestures), what vocabulary to use, and how to deal with misinterpretations or misunderstandings. Using AAC systems effectively entails much more than simply selecting words!

It is suggested that you practice communicating in specific situations with someone with whom you are comfortable. Your partner could act out the speaking person's part and you could be yourself. Or switch roles; have your partner use your AAC system to show you how he or she might communicate in that environment. Ask your partner to let you know how you are doing and then gradually try out your new skills and vocabulary in real-life situations.

UPDATING YOUR VOCABULARY REGULARLY

The words you need to communicate must reflect the changes and new situations within your life. For this reason, AAC users find that their displays and devices must express what is happening in their lives. This means that you should make arrangements to update your vocabulary on a fairly regular basis. The time you need to devote to this is an individual decision; it depends on what you already have and how much more you need. These update sessions do not need to be done with an AAC specialist or clinician. The AAC clinician can provide guidelines or a layout for expanding your AAC system. The actual selection and development of your system can usually be done by you with a family member, friend, support service provider, or another person who knows you well.

1

Directing Personal Services

This chapter lists vocabulary and tips for specific activities in the categories of general and routine services, including sample morning and evening routines. It also provides vocabulary for managing personal attendant services and addressing conflicts with your attendant, as well as violations of your rights on his or her part.

Directing your personal services is much more than having certain words available to you. It is a skill that needs to be learned. There are many excellent transitional training programs and resources to support you in learning to work with personal attendants. AAC users frequently report that they need vocabulary as well as skill training programs to assist them in developing their ability to direct their services. You may want to discuss this with your instructors so you will have the words you need to practice and use when communicating with your personal attendants.

Directing Personal Services

Suggestions	Add	Something like this
General Services Vocabulary		
I need you to		
I'd like you to		
I want some help with		
I want/I need		
Please get me		
Could you/Can you		
Would you/Why don't you		
Please do that now		
That can wait		
Can you come back?		
Look in		
Go in		
Move		
Take out		
Check		
Change		
Turn on/turn off		
Get ready/set up		
Watch out for		
Give/get/put		
Make		
Please		
Thanks		
Plan		
Be careful		

TIPS

A useful resource for directing your personal services is *Busting Loose to Independence Through Personal Attendant Services* (Nosek, 1989). This set of four excellent audiotapes contains a lot of good advice for people who are beginning to direct their services.

Audiotapes are great for many AAC users who have difficulty turning pages or reading. A variety of switches and latching devices are available to modify a tape recorder for a person who cannot manipulate the small control buttons. To find alternative ways to stop and start a tape recorder, contact your AAC service provider or local device vendor.

Suggestions	Add	Something like this
Daily Chores/ Light Housekeeping		
Empty the trash		
Empty the wastebaskets		
Pick up things/tidy up		
Do the dishes		
Wipe the counters		
Sweep		
Vacuum		
Mop the floors		
Make the bed		
Check the telephone messages		
Make a telephone call		
Set up the		
television		
computer		
book		
magazine		
music		
door opener		
alarm		
Prepare my meal/snack		
Check the refrigerator for staples		
Book/confirm transportation		
Prepare my clothes for tomorrow		
Put away		
Water the plants		
Turn on/off the lights		

TIPS

Using "Please" and "Thanks"

Know when to say "Please" and "Thank you." You will need to find your own comfort level with this. Use these words by all means, but try not to overdo it. You can risk sounding too needy when, in fact, your attendant is simply doing his or her job. Nonetheless, being polite is important and fosters a better work environment. You may want to keep words such as *please* and *thanks* set apart on your display or in your device and use them at your own discretion.

Directing Personal Services

Suggestions	Add	Something like this
Open/close the drapes/ blinds		
Pick up my mail		
Take things out of/put things into my bag		
Dust		
Clean my wheelchair tray communication device		
Shop/buy/pick up		
Make an appointment		
Write/mail a letter		
Check my money/bus tokens		
Other:		

NOTES

Suggestions	Add	Something like this
Weekly Housekeeping		
Clean the kitchen bathroom bedroom living room		
Wash/vacuum/mop the floors		
Dust the furniture		
Wash/clean the windows		
Clean the refrigerator oven stove		
Defrost the freezer		
Change the bed linens		
Clean the cupboards/closets		
Weekly shopping		
Make shopping list		
Do laundry		
Check cleaning supplies		
Other:		

TIPS

Explain Why You Want Things Done a Certain Way

Have sentences in your device or display that explain why you want things done a certain way. People are much more apt to do something your way if they understand the reason. For instance, stating that you get pressure sores from fabric wrinkles explains to your attendant why he or she should spend some extra time smoothing out your clothes and sheets.

Suggestions	Add	Something like this
Laundry		
Laundry tub		
Washer		
Dryer		
Regular/delicate		
Permanent press		
Dry flat		
Wash		
Presoak		
Sort colors		
White/dark loads		
Put the laundry in the dryer		
Iron		
Fold/put away my laundry		
Add		
soap		
bleach		
softener		
Take to the dry cleaner		
Dirty/clean clothes		
Mending		
Check pockets		
Do up buttons/zippers		
Turn inside out		
Read the washing instructions		
Clothes hamper		
Other:		

TIPS

Asking for Assistance

Rather than using the same request form over and over, you can vary how you ask for things. For example, here are different ways to ask for a drink:

- Could you get me a drink, please?
- I'd like a drink.
- When you are finished what you are doing, I'd like a drink.

Suggestions	Add	Something like this
Cooking		
Prepare/cook		
Thaw/defrost		
Microwave		
Roast		
Heat up		
Barbecue		
Bake		
Simmer		
Boil		
Broil		
Fry/stir fry		
Poach		
Scramble		
Grill		
Toast		
Cut up/chop/slice		
Purée/blend		
Steam		
Melt		
Let cool		
Chill		
Mix		
Measure		
Grate		
Whisk/beat		
Casserole		
Other:		

TIPS

Add your own favorite foods and beverages. You may want to consider the following categories:

- Appetizers
- Salads
- Soups
- Pasta
- Vegetarian main dishes
- Vegetable side dishes
- Meat
- Poultry
- Fish
- Desserts
- Snacks

Suggestions	Add	Something like this
Care of Wheelchair and Devices		
Manual wheelchair		
Power wheelchair		
Scooter		
Plug in my wheelchair battery		
Call the wheelchair repair company		
Engage/disengage the clutch		
Check the tires for air/ put air in tires		
Check the battery		
Clean my chair		
Lock/unlock the brakes		
Charge my communication device (see the "Maintaining a Communication Device" section of Chapter 4)		
Clean my tray		
Clean my communication book/device		
Call my AAC service provider		
Adjust the volume/screen		
Repairs/servicing		
Loose/torn upholstery		
Other:		

TIPS

Photographic documentation saves time you would spend describing how you want something set up. If you do not have such photographs, develop your own written setup instructions. You may want to describe how to arrange the following:

- Books
- Television and remote control
- Telephone
- Environmental controls
- Computer
- Communication device/display

Suggestions	Add	Something like this
Washing/Showering		
Bath		
Shower		
Wheel-in shower		
Bath seat		
Bench		
Shower chair		
Bed bath		
Lather		
Rinse off		
Soak		
Clean ears		
Dry		
Check the water temperature		
Too hot/cold/warm		
Towels/washcloths/sponge		
Soap		
Lotion		
Powder		
Deodorant		
Bubble bath		
Bath oil		
Close the door		
Please respect my privacy		
Take more/less time		
Brisk/quick/invigorating		
Slow/relaxing/comforting		
Wipe out tub/shower/sink		
Put away supplies		

TIPS

To ensure her privacy during bathing, Jane tells her attendant to put a lot of bubble bath in her tub and to use a thick sponge when washing her. Jane also directs her attendant to wear gloves when giving her intimate services, such as washing and toilet assistance.

Suggestions	Add	Something like this
Hair Care		
Wash my hair		
Be careful not to spray water on my face or in my ears.		
Wet hair thoroughly		
Shampoo/conditioner/gel/ hair spray		
Massage		
Rinse well		
Comb/brush		
Blow dry/towel dry		
Ask me how I want to wear my hair.		
Hairstyle (e.g., hair up, loose)		
Curling iron		
Hairdresser		
Hair salon		
Cut/trim		
Perm		
Color/highlight		
Shiny		
Manageable		
Other:		

TIPS

Some Suggestions for Directing Your Service Routines

1. Document what you want done on a daily basis. These instructions might include how you want your attendants to assist you with eating, drinking, dressing, lifting, and personal hygiene activities.
2. Indicate on these instructions when you want to be consulted. For example, you might want your attendant to ask you if you want your services given to you according to your daily instructions or whether you have any special instructions for that day. You may want your attendant to always ask you what you choose to wear and eat.
3. Make sure that your attendant knows how you communicate with and without your display and device. Body language is very important during care routines.
4. Have vocabulary ready for different contexts (e.g., grocery shopping, booking transportation, booking attendant services).

These directions for routine service should be given to the agency supervisor and the primary attendant, and a copy can be kept in a binder in your room.

Suggestions	Add	Something like this
Shaving		
Razor		
Electric shaver		
Blade		
Shaving cream		
Gel		
Aftershave		
Cologne		
Shave my face		
Shave my legs		
Shave my underarms		
New blade		
Old/dull blade		
Wax		
Hair remover		
Moisture cream		
Lotion		
Beard trimmer		
Mustache trimmer		
Careful! Don't cut me.		
Plastic bandage		
Wash the razor		
Change the blade		
Keep my skin taut when shaving me.		
Other:		

TIPS

Maria has arranged that her attendant uses a checklist of things to do before leaving Maria's room.

- Check that my call bell, television controls, and door opener are within reach.
- Ask if I want a drink, need the bed raised or lowered, or want to communicate something else with my display.

Suggestions	Add	Something like this
Dental Care		
Toothbrush		
Electric toothbrush		
Toothpaste		
Inside/outside of my gums		
Teeth		
Gums		
Dentures		
Floss		
Rinse		
Use gentle strokes		
Mouthwash		
Toothache		
Sensitive gums		
Call my dentist at		
Checkup		
Other:		

TIPS

AAC users often stress the importance of communicating effectively with their attendants.

Communicating Matters: A Training Guide for Personal Attendants Working with Consumers Who Have Enhanced Communication Needs (Collier, 2000) is a videotape training program for personal attendants working with people who have enhanced communication needs. People with enhanced communication needs require assistance from their partners in order to communicate their messages effectively. They might not be able to point independently to the needed words or letters, or they might rely on pictures or symbols because they are not able to spell everything they need to communicate.

The video and its manual address the following:

- How AAC users communicate
- The impact of having enhanced communication needs
- Strategies that attendants can use during service routines

Suggestions	Add	Something like this
Nail Care		
Toenails		
Fingernails		
Clip my nails		
Cut my nails		
Clean under my nails		
Keep my nails short		
Let my nails grow		
Shape my nails		
File my nails		
Paint my nails		
Remove my nail polish		
Smooth the edges		
Push the cuticle back gently		
Dry between my toes		
Other:		

TIPS

Scott uses the following instructions when telling a new attendant how to cut his nails:

When cutting or cleaning my nails, it is important to understand that my hand may clench. This is due to spasticity.

It does not help to tell me to relax or open my hand. I cannot control it.

The best procedure follows:

- Gently pry open each finger.
- Hold each finger when you cut or clean the nail.
- Cut the nails short.
- File any jagged nails so I won't scratch myself.

Thank you.

Suggestions	Add	Something like this
Makeup		
Cleanser		
Moisturizer		
Foundation		
Perfume		
Eyeshadow		
Eyeliner		
Mascara		
Blush		
Powder		
Lipstick		
Lip gloss		
Blend		
Use a damp sponge.		
Show me my choices.		
Too heavy		
Please take it off.		
Please put more on.		
Put a towel over my shoulders to protect my clothes.		
Other:		

TIPS

Cindy's face begins to spasm when her attendant applies Cindy's makeup. When this happens, Cindy's attendant puts her fingers gently on Cindy's cheekbones and rests them there until the spasm subsides.

Suggestions	Add	Something like this
Bathroom		
Toilet		
Bedpan		
Urinal		
Commode		
Toilet paper/wipes		
Washcloth/water/soap		
Protectors for bed		
Urine		
Bowel movement		
Bowel routine		
Condom catheter		
Intermittent catheterization		
Indwelling catheter		
Suprapubic catheter		
Ileal conduit		
Suppository		
Digital stimulation		
Enema		
Disimpaction		
Colostomy		
Leg bag		
Leg bag strap		
Night bag		
Gas		
Infection		
Briefs		
Clean undergarments		

TIPS

Bill has written these instructions to tell his attendants how he wants to be transferred from his bed to his chair:

1. Get the lift in the bathroom. Put it beside my bed.
2. Set up my wheelchair beside my bed. Lock the brakes.
3. Turn me on my side.
4. Put the cloth sling under my mid-section.
5. Connect the chains to the cloth sling. Short chains connect at the shoulder, longer ones at the knees.
6. Pump the lift's handle until I am raised off of the bed.
7. Swing me over to my wheelchair.
8. Push my knees back as you lower me. This helps control my movement.
9. When you are ready to lower me, open the lift's valve slowly by turning the knob.
10. When I am lowered, lean me forward to remove the straps.

Suggestions	Add	Something like this
Shields/underpads		
I need to be excused.		
I need some assistance in the washroom.		
I can manage on my own.		
I would like a woman/man to assist me.		
Please wait here/outside.		
Rearrange my clothing		
Empty and clean/rinse		
Please respect my privacy.		
I'll call when I'm ready.		
Can you come back in _______ minutes?		
Other:		

TIPS

Anne uses these instructions to tell her attendants how she wants to be repositioned in bed:

1. Put a pillow under my right hip.
2. Ask me which way I want to lie down. I'll use my eyes to direct you.
3. When moving me, first move my hips and my bottom. Then move my shoulders.

Suggestions	Add	Something like this
Feminine Hygiene		
Period		
Tampon		
Sanitary napkin		
Pad		
Panty liner		
Heavy		
Light		
Spotting		
Cramps		
Back pain		
Headache		
Premenstrual syndrome (PMS)		
Medication		
Other:		

NOTES

Suggestions	Add	Something like this
Skin Care		
Bedsores		
Pressure sores from sitting from wrinkled clothing		
Sharp/dull pain		
Redness/rash/bruise		
Sore/cut/scratch/blister		
Itching/burning		
Dry/flaky skin		
Skin breakdown		
Change position		
Put a pillow		
Pressure/heating pad		
Straighten my clothing/ sheets		
Loosen my clothing/bedding		
Waterbed		
Sheepskin		
Mattress cover		
Other:		

TIPS

Jill has documented how she wants to be assisted when dressing:

- I usually select what I want to wear the night before.
- Ask me if I want to change any of my selections. If I say yes, give me choices.
- When dressing me,
  1. Cover the naked parts of my body with a sheet.
  2. Put on my top first. Pull it over my head. Put my left arm in the sleeve. Then put my right arm in the other sleeve.
  3. Ask me if I want my top tucked in.
  4. Put on my pants.
  5. Put on my socks. Ask me if I want them rolled down or pulled up.
  6. Straighten my clothes, and check for wrinkles in the fabric.

Suggestions	Add	Something like this
Eating and Drinking		
Use a regular/my own fork/ spoon		
Use a regular/my own dish		
Use a regular/my own straw		
Use plate guards/nonslip mats		
Use a clothing protector		
Wait until I am finished swallowing		
I'll look at you/the plate when I'm ready for more.		
Wash your hands		
Wear/do not wear latex gloves		
I'm allergic to latex; please do not wear latex gloves.		
I'll look at the cup when I want a drink.		
Go slower/faster		
Wipe my mouth		
Check the temperature		
Cut up my food		
Bite-size		
Smaller/larger mouthfuls		
I like/don't like that.		
I want more.		
I'm finished.		
Other:		

TIPS

Matthew has documented the following instructions to tell his attendant how to assist him when drinking:

1. Use a plastic cup.
2. Put a towel around my neck.
3. Stand on my right side.
4. Hold the cup in front of my mouth.
5. Hold a paper towel under my chin.
6. Put the cup on my lower lip. Wait for me to bite down on the edge.
7. Tilt the cup.
8. Let me swallow twice, then take the cup away.
9. I'll look at the cup if I want more.
10. Sometimes I cough when swallowing. Please don't worry if this happens.

Suggestions	Add	Something like this
Common Illnesses		
Sick		
Cold/flu		
Cough		
I need help with coughing.		
Allergies		
Infection		
Perspiration		
Fever		
Take temperature		
Headache		
Shaking/goose bumps		
Runny nose		
Stuffy nose/congested		
Nausea		
Dull/sharp pain		
Cramp		
Spasm		
Ache		
Stiff		
Tired/no energy		
Upset stomach		
Constipation		
Diarrhea/"the runs"		
Increased fluids		
Medication		
Bed rest		
Medical attention		

NOTES

Suggestions	Add	Something like this
Making Appointments/ Bookings for Attendant Services		
I would like to make/book an appointment.		
I need to cancel my appointment/booking.		
I need an appointment/a booking for meal preparation daily activities		
Is anyone available?		
I need an appointment/a booking for 10, 15, or 30 minutes.		
Prebooking		
I want to make a change to my scheduled appointment/booking.		
Downtime		
Schedule/reschedule		
Appointment/booking sheets		
When are my appointments/ bookings?		
Who is on that shift?		
I want a male/female attendant.		
Other:		

TIPS

Every agency has its own procedures for making or booking attendant services. You will need to select appropriate vocabulary to negotiate your service schedules or to make changes to your routines.

Suggestions	Add	Something like this
Giving Feedback to Attendants		
Thank you		
Sure/okay		
Excellent		
That's great		
Perfect		
Good		
Wonderful		
All right		
You did really well.		
Good job		
Well done		
I don't like that because		
I decided that		
I changed my mind.		
Keep trying—it'll get easier.		
Don't lose heart.		
Practice makes perfect.		
Please go slower/faster.		
Please be more gentle.		
You won't/will hurt me.		
You just need to relax.		
You probably don't mean it, but		
Is it okay with you if		
It upsets me when you tell me what to do don't ask my opinion talk to me like that treat me like that		

TIPS

Giving Feedback to Attendants

It is important to let attendants know how well or how poorly they are performing their work.

Positive feedback is just as important—if not more important—than negative feedback.

Try to give constructive criticism.

Communicate about how a task could have been done better. For example, you might say, "I don't like that. I'm afraid my hip will be injured. Be gentle and go slowly."

When giving positive feedback, you may want to tell your attendant why you thought he or she did a good job, such as "Great! You did that very gently."

The vocabulary in this chapter can be adjusted for speaking with others in many different situations.

Suggestions	Add	Something like this
You're having some trouble with the first/middle/last part.		
I think it might be good for you to see someone else do it.		
I want you to do it this way.		
That doesn't feel quite right.		
Please don't do that.		
I'm uncomfortable.		
Could you do that again?		
That's not the way I want it.		
Please follow my instructions.		
I'm not happy with that.		
That was too slow fast rough		
I don't want to do that.		
I can't do that.		
Can we do this later?		
Please take your time.		
Other:		

TIPS

Learning to Communicate During Service Routines

Areas in which some AAC users may need assistance are the following:

- Developing individual service routines
- Teaching attendants to communicate more effectively with AAC users
- Acquiring vocabulary for specific service routines
- Negotiating service contracts

(Collier, 1999)

SAMPLE MORNING AND EVENING ROUTINES

As everyone has his or her own unique needs, you must develop a morning and evening routine that suits you. The following sample routines have been contributed by Don. He has set up a strict service routine to avoid communicating the same details every day. As a result, Don's attendant can spend more time on his services and the work that he needs done and less time duplicating previous communications. Don gives a typed copy of his routine to new attendants so they can follow his instructions step by step. He uses his display and device to communicate specific information, such as an unusual job he wants done or a special event for which he needs to prepare.

Sample Morning Routine

1. Clear bedside table. Put everything back to where it should be. Ask me if you are not sure where things go. I will use my eyes to show you where they go.
2. Disconnect the charging cord from my electric wheelchair and connect the battery to the chair (the red dots match up).
3. Turn on the electric teapot, which is on the kitchen counter.
4. Disconnect the light-switch cord, headphones, and urinal from the bed rail.
5. Raise the whole bed as high as it will go. The switch is on the right-hand side of the bed rail.
6. Fill two basins with warm water and place them on the bedside table. One is for washing, the other is for rinsing off the soap.

TIPS

Don includes photographs in his routine instructions to show his attendants how he likes things to be done.

7. Get the washcloth from the washroom and two towels from the clothes cupboard.
8. Get the soap, aftershave, and moisturizing lotion from the washroom. If any of these items need to be replaced, check the cupboard under the sink.
9. Wash my face and hands with soap and water. Apply aftershave to my face and lotion to my hands.
10. Get clean water.
11. Wash the rest of my body and apply lotion.
12. Cover me with sheets.
13. Clean the bowls and washcloth and leave them in the washroom.
14. Clean the bedside table with a dishcloth from the kitchen sink.
15. Return the television controls, door opener, communication display, and telephone to the bedside table.
16. Dress me in a clean T-shirt, sweater, pants, socks, and shoes (see the photograph that illustrates how to do this).
17. Make sure all clothes are straight and not off to one side.
18. Put on my watch.
19. Position the wheelchair for transfer (see photograph).
20. Use the mechanical lift to transfer me (see photograph).
21. Clean and put on my glasses.
22. Brush my teeth at the washroom basin.
23. Fasten my wheelchair's waist belt.
24. Make the bed.
25. Plug in the electric razor. I will shave myself later.

TIPS

Like many AAC users, Don has a number of attendants who assist him with his daily routines. He insists that they keep things in the same place. This makes it easier for him to tell other attendants where to get the things he needs.

26. Ask me if there are any small jobs to be done.

Sample Evening Routine

1. Prepare my snack and meal.
2. Place my drink and food on my bedside table.
3. Get out clean clothes for tomorrow. Let me choose my clothes. Hold up suggestions and I will nod "yes" or shake my head "no."
4. Ask me if there are any small jobs to be done. I will use my device or display to answer and provide details.
5. Wash my face and hands with the washcloth from the cupboard.
6. Leave the washcloth out for tomorrow.
7. Comb my hair.
8. Empty the urinal in the washroom and connect it back on the bed rail.
9. Pull the bedcovers down.
10. Put the blue pad on the mattress.
11. Put the beige cushion in the middle of the bed.
12. Move the bed closer to the floor. That will make it easier to transfer me.
13. Get the mechanical lift from the other room.
14. Open any shirt buttons. Lift my right arm and pull the back of my shirt over my head (see photograph).
15. Put the cloth sling under my midsection (see photograph).
16. Tilt the wheelchair back a little and remove my clothes.
17. Connect the lift's chains to the cloth sling. The short ones connect at the shoulder; the longer ones connect at

NOTES

the knees (illustrated with a photograph).

18. Transfer me to the bed.
19. Put the beige cushion under my knees (see photograph).
20. Raise the bed to the highest level.
21. Remove the sling.
22. Wash and dry me.
23. Apply lotion to my hands.
24. Cover me with the bedcovers.
25. Raise the bed rails.
26. Attach the string from the light switch over my bed to the bed rail on my right.
27. Make sure that the television controls, door opener, communication display, and telephone are on my bedside table.
28. Pull the bedside table close to the bed (see photograph).
29. Charge my electric wheelchair.
30. Charge my communication device.
31. Turn on the air mattress at the foot of the bed.
32. Make sure that all windows and drapes are closed.
33. Set the security system as you leave.
34. Lock the door, and close it tightly behind you.

NOTES

Suggestions	Add	Something like this
Services		
Service agency		
Project		
Co-op		
Support services		
Outreach attendant services		
Self-managed		
Direct		
Supportive housing		
24-hour attendant services		
Purchased services		
Fee for service		
Shared service		
Time-sharing		
Organization		
Live-in		
Individualized funding		
Client-centered service		
Homemaking		
Other:		

TIPS

There are many different types of housing options, employment and educational environments, and support service models, and each has its own set of vocabulary and terms.

Some of this terminology is listed here so you can participate in conversations and negotiations regarding your support services needs.

Remember, these are only ideas. You should add words that reflect your situation.

Suggestions	Add	Something like this
Environments		
Home		
Group home		
Apartment		
Shared accommodation		
Nursing home		
Institution		
Hospital		
Enhanced-support services		
Family home		
Workplace		
Sheltered workshop		
Supported employment		
Competitive employment		
Self-employment		
Part-time employment		
Educational program		
Literacy program		
Volunteer program		
Day program		
Rehabilitation program		
Clinic		
Other:		

NOTES

Directing Personal Services

Suggestions	Add	Something like this
People		
Family		
Friend		
Advocate		
Network		
Resident		
Tenant		
Consumer/client		
Augmentative and alternative communication (AAC) user		
Disabled		
Physically challenged		
Handicapped		
Nondisabled		
Staff		
Attendant/personal assistant		
Same-sex attendant		
Service provider		
Coordinator		
Supervisor		
Volunteer		
Project manager		
Director		
Facilitator		
Team		
Self-help group		
Peer support group		
Support group		

TIPS

Managing your support services entails having the words you need as well as the skills to use them effectively.

Suggestions	Add	Something like this
Service Contracts		
Service agreement/plan		
Consumer rights		
Responsibilities		
Give/refuse consent		
Signed consent		
Participate in		
Authorize		
Develop/review/evaluate		
Laws/rules/policies/ guidelines		
Designated decision maker		
Direct services		
Documentation		
Accommodate changes/ needs		
Contingency plan		
Cancellation		
Hospitalization		
Eligibility		
Conditions		
Duration		
Complaint process		
Accountability		
Renew contract		
Terminate contract		
Negotiate contract		
Other:		

TIPS

How you receive your services varies considerably from place to place. This list includes some vocabulary that AAC users have found helpful in negotiating their service contracts.

Suggestions	Add	Something like this
Rights		
Respect		
Courtesy		
Treats me like an adult		
Sensitive to my feelings		
Acts promptly		
Takes my opinions seriously		
Safe/secure		
Free from abuse		
Respect for my dignity privacy autonomy		
Make decisions		
Information		
Personal requirements/ needs		
Confidential		
Other:		

TIPS

Do you know your rights?

Do you know when they have been violated?

Do you know what to do if you think one of your rights is not being respected?

Contact your local consumer organization for information. Ask for an explanation of your rights and an interpretation of what these rights mean in your daily life.

Suggestions	Add	Something like this
Dealing with Conflicts and Violations		
Mental abuse		
intimidate		
make fun of		
make feel incompetent		
undue criticism		
"silent treatment"		
threaten		
Physical abuse		
beat		
hurt		
injure		
bruise		
grab		
hit		
rough handling		
withhold basic needs		
neglect		
Sexual abuse (see Chapter 16, "Sexuality")		
Financial abuse		
steal		
damage property		
mismanage money		
Complaint process		
Register a complaint		
Time off		
Replacement		
Negotiate/discuss		
Conflict		
Problem		
Find common ground		
Independence/dependence		

TIPS

Dealing with Conflicts

There are a number of excellent training programs to help you deal with situations of conflict.

Here are some general hints:

1. State the problem.
   Decide how you will communicate your message with the vocabulary available to you. Prepare your message in your device or on your computer. Rehearse. Be direct and to the point. For example, if your attendant is consistently showing up late, you might want to approach this problem by stating, "Our agreement is that you will put me to bed at 10:30 P.M. every night. You have been arriving between 11:00 P.M. and 11:30 P.M. for the past week. Can we discuss this?"
2. The attendant will give his or her side of the story.
3. You need to make some comments at this point. You may want to address the following topics:
   - The fact that this is not acceptable to you
   - The reason why it is not acceptable
   - Inviting the attendant to think of ways to address the problem (e.g., asking "What can we do about this?")

(*continued on page 42*)

Directing Personal Services

Suggestions	Add	Something like this
Motivation		
Good attitude/bad attitude		
Reliable/unreliable		
Satisfactory/unsatisfactory		
Reasonable/unreasonable		
Acceptable/unacceptable		
Trained/untrained		
Positive/negative		
Confident/not confident		
Competent/incompetent		
Permanent/temporary		
Full-time/part-time		
Overprotective		
Honest/dishonest		
Trustworthy/not trustworthy		
Abuse/abusive		
Respect/disrespect		
Flexible/inflexible		
Willing/unwilling		
Sensitive/insensitive		
Considerate/inconsiderate		
Experienced/inexperienced		
Violation		
Grounds for termination		
Other:		

TIPS

4. Prepare some solutions to discuss. Present your best solution first. Get a response from your attendant before making other suggestions.
5. Once a solution has been agreed on, you may want to suggest that you and your attendant set a date to evaluate its effectiveness.

2

Participating in Service Meetings

As health care services become more consumer and family oriented, many augmentative and alternative communication (AAC) users attend and participate in their own service meetings. These meetings are usually initiated by a health care professional, but you can and should feel free to request meetings whenever you think there is a need to coordinate your services with your service providers.

Who is invited to attend the meeting depends on the meeting's focus. Many AAC users have a number of service providers and deal with different service agencies. Thus, regular team meetings are necessary for keeping people informed and coordinating your services. Many AAC users believe it is important to participate actively in setting their own goals and discussing ways in which these goals can be achieved. This chapter, therefore, suggests vocabulary for planning a meeting, setting the agenda, participating in discussions, and developing action plans. Some of this vocabulary comes from The Aphasia Centre–North York, Ontario, Canada (see Appendix B for more information).

Suggestions	Add	Something like this
Planning the Meeting		
When is the meeting?		
Where is the meeting?		
Who is invited?		
I want to invite my family physiotherapist speech-language pathologist social worker occupational therapist doctor nurse recreational therapist attendant friend educator employer AAC clinician Others:		
Who will direct the meeting?		
Who will take notes?		
What will be discussed?		
Other:		

TIPS

Participating in Your Service Meetings

You have the right to say who should attend your service meetings.

It is important to include people who need to know various aspects of your service.

Consider preparing a response scale to use during meetings. This can be a good way to provide quick feedback on discussion points. Decide on the wording you want, and make sure that the scale is set up in such a way that you have access to it. The scale might contain some of the following responses:

- I agree.
- I need to think about it.
- I'm not comfortable with that.
- I disagree.

Also see Chapter 15, "Participating at a Convention," for suggestions on communicating in group discussions.

Suggestions	Add	Something like this
Setting the Agenda		
I want to discuss		
I want to know about		
I have concerns about		
I have questions about		
I need help with		
family matters		
my progress		
my goals		
communication		
occupational therapy		
physiotherapy		
employment/work		
education		
transportation		
medication		
seating		
my computer		
my communication device/display		
environmental controls		
attendant support services		
my residence		
money		
my schedule		
plans for when I am sick		
Other:		

TIPS

Remember that the job of your health care providers is to assist you.

Prepare your concerns and questions in advance. You might want to forward them to the meeting chairperson ahead of time so an agenda can be developed to address everyone's discussion points. In turn, the chairperson might inform other team members of your issues. This would allow them to consider your needs before the meeting and, thus, to formulate some suggestions.

Ask to have a copy of the notes or minutes sent to you and everyone who attended the meeting.

If anything is to be done after the meeting, make sure that you know on what time lines they will operate and how everyone will communicate with each other in the future.

Suggestions	Add	Something like this
Participating in Discussions		
That is important/not important to me.		
That might be an issue in the future.		
I'm pleased with		
I don't know/I know.		
I don't understand/I understand.		
Maybe		
Let's try it.		
Let's review that in		
What do you think?		
I need time to think about it.		
I don't want that.		
Sounds good		
Can we discuss this at another meeting?		
We need more information.		
Other:		

TIPS

Some people refrain from bringing up certain issues at meetings because the "right" people are not in attendance. Do not let this stop you from raising such issues. For instance, if communication is your concern and a speech-language pathologist is not available, or if you want environmental controls and you do not have access to anyone who can help you in this area, you should still state the problem. Your service team can assist you in finding appropriate services if they know about your needs.

Suggestions	Add	Something like this
Developing Action Plans		
Who will do that?		
What are we trying to achieve?		
How will we do that?		
Let's develop a plan.		
I want to receive copies of all reports relating to my service.		
I would like copies of all reports to go to		
When will that be done?		
Please write that down in my journal.		
Please call		
Please talk with		
When can we meet to follow up on this plan?		
Other:		

NOTES

3

Interviewing Service Providers

As discussed in the previous chapter on participating in service meetings, people who use augmentative and alternative communication (AAC) often want their service providers to work as a team so that services can be coordinated. Many AAC users also want to be included in any team decisions relating to their lives and service. It is a good idea to discuss these expectations if your team members change or if you are just starting with a new team.

The training and experience of your service providers directly affect you and your services. You have the right to ask questions about their qualifications, experience, and work philosophy. You can do this in a nonconfrontational way. This chapter suggests vocabulary for hiring or getting to know both an assistant and a health care professional.

Suggestions	Add	Something like this
Hiring and/or Getting to Know an Assistant		
Tell me about yourself.		
What kinds of jobs have you had in the past?		
How long have you been with this agency?		
Do you have experience working with people with disabilities?		
Do you have experience working with someone who uses AAC?		
Do you know anyone with a disability?		
Do you drive? What is your driving record like?		
Do you have a police record?		
Are you willing to be somewhat flexible about schedules?		
Do you have any hearing or vision problems?		
Have you ever had back problems?		
Can you lift weights of up to ______ pounds?		
Please read this aloud so I can check your reading skills.		
Have you ever attended any training programs? If yes, which programs?		

TIPS

Interviewing Service Providers

Use these questions as guidelines to develop ones that reflect your needs and situation.

Some of these phrases might be useful if you want to hire someone to do something for you. You should tailor your questions to the task and the amount of responsibility involved.

If you use an AAC system that relies on your partner's having to read the words you communicate, make sure that a prospective service provider has no difficulty seeing and reading the language in which you communicate.

Suggestions	Add	Something like this
Please give me the names, addresses, and telephone numbers of three people to serve as references.		
Do you have any questions?		
I will need to check your references.		
I think/don't think this position is for you.		
Other:		

NOTES

Suggestions	Add	Something like this
Interviewing Health Care Professionals		
What are your qualifications?		
Have you taken any specialized training courses?		
What is your background/ discipline?		
Do you work alone or as part of a team?		
What is the background of the other members on your team?		
To what professional organizations do you belong?		
May I see proof of membership?		
Are you a member of the International Society of Augmentative and Alternative Communication (ISAAC)?		
Are you a member of a local ISAAC chapter or group?		
Do you read any special journals/publications about AAC?		
Is your service covered by ______ ?		
What is the fee for your service?		
I'd like to be involved in all decisions regarding my service.		

TIPS

In some countries and/or states, there is an accreditation process for AAC service providers. This means that accredited service providers have met certain standards of practice.

AAC service providers may include speech-language pathologists, occupational therapists, and rehabilitation technologists. AAC experience and training may vary greatly, depending on the service organization as well as the individual who is providing your services.

Find out about AAC services in your area by contacting government, consumer, and professional organizations.

Suggestions	Add	Something like this
I'd like you to work closely with		
What services can I expect from you?		
I want to be involved in developing my service priorities and plans.		
What is the service plan?		
What are the time lines?		
What are my responsibilities?		
Can we develop a service contract?		
Other:		

TIPS

A service plan might include

- A definition of your goal(s)
- An action plan to address your goal(s)
- A projected date for the completion of each action
- A designated person to address each action within the plan
- A time to review your goal(s) and the process

4

Communicating About Your Communication System

Augmentative and alternative communication (AAC) users report that they want to make informed decisions when selecting, purchasing, or leasing communication devices. They also want to have input on the setup and vocabulary of their AAC systems. In addition, they want to be able to give clear instructions to their attendants as to how to care for and maintain their AAC systems.

This chapter provides vocabulary and tips for people who use communication devices, communication displays, or computers/writing systems to communicate. Specific issues addressed for communication devices include maintaining a voice output communication aid (VOCA) and leasing, renting, and purchasing a device. In terms of communication displays, adding and deleting vocabulary and using trays/mounts are discussed. Regarding computers/writing systems, vocabulary is suggested for hardware, pointing devices and keyboards, software, and common problems.

Communicating About Your Communication System

Suggestions	Add	Something like this
Selecting an AAC Device		
Please show me all of my options.		
Where can I see other devices?		
Can I meet someone who uses this device?		
What are my options for operating this device?		
What are my options for representing my vocabulary on this device?		
How clear is the voice?		
Is there any research on how well people understand this voice?		
Does this device have any rate/speed enhancements that allow me to communicate more quickly?		
What is the repair record for this device?		
What is the most frequent repair problem?		
How long do repairs usually take?		
Will I get a replacement device during repairs?		
How can I back up my programs and files?		
How will it be mounted?		
How will it be charged on my manual and/or electric wheelchair?		

NOTES

Suggestions	Add	Something like this
Is it compatible with my other software programs and devices?		
What do I need to learn in order to use this device effectively?		
How long will it take to learn to use this device?		
Who will give me training on the device?		
How much training will I get?		
How many people do you know who use this device?		
Can I use this device for a trial period before I decide about purchasing it?		
Other:		

NOTES

Suggestions	Add	Something like this
Maintaining a Communication Device		
Please charge my communication device.		
Charge my device overnight.		
Unplug my communication device.		
Please check the battery level.		
Check the manual for charging instructions.		
Please clean my communication device.		
Check the manual for cleaning instructions.		
Use a soft, damp, lint-free cloth		
Please check the photograph to see how to set up my device.		
Connect all wires/cables		
Match up the colored dots		
Adjust the volume screen voice speed pitch		
Turn it on/off		
Press the switch at the back/ on the side		
AC adapter/external/ internal battery		
Light on/off		

TIPS

You need to know the following about maintaining your communication device:

- Daily care and setup routines
- Troubleshooting (for minor problems)
- Who to contact for major problems

Contact your AAC service provider or vendor if you have any concerns about these issues.

Suggestions	Add	Something like this
Plug it in		
Check the settings		
Adjust the settings (e.g., scan rate, pattern)		
Put that word or sentence in my device.		
Can you make this word sound better?		
Write that down so I can copy it.		
Do the programming with/ for me.		
Ask me where I want you to put the words and phrases.		
Go over some of my vocabulary locations with me.		
Put these words into a sentence for me.		
Save the vocabulary.		
Make a new page.		
Change the location of that item.		
Change the picture that goes with that word.		
Adjust the position of the switch.		
Check that the switch is working.		
There is a problem with the switch. It is sticking unreliable too slow too sensitive		

TIPS

Depending on the type of device you utilize, some of these suggestions may or may not be appropriate.

Decide which words and phrases you need to tell your attendant how to set up your device on a daily basis.

Suggestions	Add	Something like this
Leasing or Purchasing a System		
Can I lease this?		
Can I purchase this?		
How much will it cost?		
What does that mean?		
Please explain that in every-day language.		
Give me an example.		
I don't understand/I understand.		
Could you speak more slowly?		
Please repeat that.		
How often do I need to pay that amount?		
Is it a better deal if I purchase it?		
Third-party funding		
The name of your funding source		
Do you know how I can get help funding my portion?		
How much will the third party pay?		
Who owns the device?		
Will I ever own the leased device?		
What happens if I can't make a payment?		
How much time will I have to make payments?		

TIPS

Access to funding sources for leasing or purchasing a communication device may depend on where you live.

If you do receive funding, there may be specific criteria for purchasing or leasing a device. In addition, it may be necessary to complete complicated forms. Do not be afraid to ask questions about anything you need explained.

Suggestions	Add	Something like this
Who is responsible for the maintenance of the device?		
What happens if it breaks down?		
Who will look after the warranties?		
Is it insured?		
What happens if I drop it?		
What happens if it is stolen or lost?		
Will my insurance company pay for a stolen or lost device?		
When can I get a new device?		
Will this affect my eligibility for another device?		
What happens if my attendant does not charge my device?		
Can I take my device out of the country?		
When can I get a new device?		
Can I get other software?		
Can I get an upgrade for the software? How much will that cost?		
How and when can I terminate the lease?		
Can I use this device at work/college?		

TIPS

It is very important that you understand your lease documents. If necessary, ask your AAC clinician to explain each point.

Communicating About Your Communication System

Suggestions	Add	Something like this
I am concerned about finances responsibility security leasing purchasing warranties repairs mounting the device training for use of the device		
Do I need to look for funding every year?		
Will the system be set up in my home?		
Will I receive training for using the system?		
Will I get help with repairs?		
Will I need to pay for repairs?		
When is the first payment due?		
Other:		

NOTES

Leasing or Purchasing a System

Suggestions	Add	Something like this
Adding/Deleting Vocabulary		
Please add that word to my display/device.		
Please write that in my notebook.		
I want to choose a picture or symbol for that word.		
Please put that in my communication binder.		
I need a new page for that situation in my display.		
I need a new display.		
I'd like to set up a regular time for you to add words to my display.		
Please delete/erase that word from my display/device.		
Clean my display/device.		
I want to pick a picture for that word.		
Where do you suggest that word could go?		
I will show you where I want you to add it.		
Please write that down, and I will copy it into my device.		
Other:		

TIPS

Communication displays are never complete. They need constant updating to reflect changes in your life.

Most AAC users have a frequently used vocabulary display (usually on their wheelchair trays) and a binder or book of vocabulary for specific situations or topics.

Make sure that you have space (especially in your binder) for new words and phrases.

It is a good idea to keep a notepad at the back of your binder or hanging from the side of your tray so you can ask people to write down any words you think you need.

Depending on how much vocabulary you are likely to gather, you should arrange periodically to have someone assist you in putting the words from your notebook into your binder or onto your frequently used vocabulary display.

Suggestions	Add	Something like this
Trays/Mounts		
Put on/take off my tray/ mount.		
Check the photograph for the correct positioning of my tray/display/device.		
Tray		
Side tray		
Lexian cover		
Swing-away		
Armrests		
Strap/belt		
Alan keys		
Tighten		
Straighten		
Move up/down/forward/ backward/left/right		
Tilt/angle		
Other:		

NOTES

Suggestions	Add	Something like this
Hardware		
Macintosh		
IBM/IBM compatible		
Power cord		
CPU		
Disk/floppy disk		
Monitor		
Printer		
Hard drive		
Memory: RAM/hard disk		
Floppy disk drive		
PC card		
Scanner		
CD-ROM		
Modem		
Fax		
Sound card		
Internet/web site		
E-mail		
Power adapter		
Power plug		
Laptop/desktop		
Battery		
Power level/charge		
On/off key		
Brightness control		
Speech output		
Speakers		
Infrared		

TIPS

Many AAC users employ computers for writing, and some employ computers for both writing and conversation.

Computer technology involves its own vocabulary. Some terms are included here. Just pick the ones you need in order to communicate effectively with your AAC service provider, tutor, employer, and others. If needed, select additional words from your systems and software manuals.

Check out these sections as well (also found in this chapter):

- "Maintaining a Communication Device"
- "Leasing or Purchasing a System"

Communicating About Your Communication System

Suggestions	Add	Something like this
Pointing Devices		
Mouse		
Trackpad/trackpoint		
Trackball		
Mouse buttons		
Adjust mouse functions		
Joystick		
Other:		
Keyboards		
Keyguard		
Keys		
Regular keyboard		
Mini/expanded keyboard		
On-screen keyboard		
Other:		

NOTES

Suggestions	Add	Something like this
Software		
Install		
Application program		
File/folder		
Backup		
Download		
Utilities		
Shareware		
Access software		
Driver		
Dialogue boxes		
Scanning		
Rate enhancement		
Word prediction		
Abbreviation/expansion		
Word processor		
Icons/graphics		
Other:		

TIPS

You may need specific vocabulary that refers to the software you use. For instance, if you use Microsoft Word, you may need to communicate about the functions that appear in the dialogue boxes (e.g., insert page break).

Whenever possible, demonstrate what you are trying to communicate. This is often the most effective way of conveying information.

Suggestions	Add	Something like this
Problems		
There's not enough memory.		
The file can't be found.		
The screen went blank.		
It froze/crashed.		
There was an error message.		
The computer shuts down.		
This function/program won't work.		
The device won't hold its charge.		
The computer won't read a disk.		
The computer/program suddenly quits.		
I can't shut down the computer.		
The disk won't eject.		
Could you call		
There's a problem with		
Could you install		
I'm concerned about		
I don't know how to use		
Please show me		
Other:		

TIPS

Ask your AAC service to give you specifications for your computer setup. That way, you will have a copy of the correct specifications should something go wrong.

Make sure that you have a list of all the software and utilities you use. For example, you might have a trackball and a talking word processor.

Because computer manuals can be difficult to follow, some AAC services will document simple instructions for operating your computer. Make sure that you keep these instructions near your computer.

When a problem occurs, try to remember what you were doing. This information is useful for your AAC service provider if the problem persists.

5

Seating

If you use a wheelchair, you may need vocabulary to communicate your needs and concerns during a seating assessment or when communicating with a vendor. Prepare for this ahead of time. This chapter gives suggested vocabulary for common seating problems as well as repairs and modifications to improve seating. Also consider using photographs, which often show seating problems very clearly, to illustrate your concerns.

Seating

Suggestions	Add	Something like this
Seating Problems		
I am having a problem with my		
insert/molded support		
chair back		
headrest		
neckrest		
brakes		
wheels		
tray		
battery		
controls		
steering		
gears		
chair angle		
chair height		
reclining/tilt mechanism		
straps/belts		
footrests		
padding		
wing		
armrests		
tires		
front caster		
joystick		
controls		
scanner		
mounting system		
push/hand grip		
spokes		
side panel		
wheel/hand rims		
antitipping lever		
cross brace		
I keep shifting in this seat.		
It's uncomfortable when I move.		

TIPS

Wheelchair Parts

Back:

- May recline, be plain, be padded, or have a special back support

Armrests:

- Usually detachable
- Might be molded

Seat:

- Usually has a cushion

Front rigging:

- Usually supports foot pedals

Foot pedals:

- May swing away or be detachable
- Might have toe straps
- Might elevate

Suggestions	Add	Something like this
Too small/too large		
Too tight/too loose		
I can't put on my winter coat while sitting in this chair.		
The tray is too hard too high too low not secure		
Swing away		
Detachable		
Fixed		
Comfortable/uncomfortable		
Broken		
Unreliable		
Inconsistent		
Unsafe		
Slides		
Slump		
Gets caught		
Needs repositioning		
I have pain/cramps/stiffness in my upper back/shoulder arms/elbows/hands bottom lower back/hip legs/feet neck/head		
Other:		

TIPS

Have someone take a photograph to show a typical problem you encounter with your seating (e.g., slumping down in the seat, getting stuck behind the insert). This will make it easier for your seating clinician to understand the problem.

Seating

Suggestions	Add	Something like this
Repairs and Modifications		
Can you adjust		
Does it need to be replaced?		
The tires may need air.		
The battery is low.		
The tilt/recline mechanism is not working properly.		
The speed is too slow/too fast.		
The steering is off.		
Can you change the speed?		
It's running out of power.		
Can you repair it?		
Do I need a new one?		
Please change the angle height position support shape softness tightness/looseness		
I think it might be better if		
What do you think?		
Can I try it?		
Can you check it out?		
I don't know until I try.		
Build up		
Take down/out		
Pull up		
Raise/lower		
Support		

TIPS

Use a diagram to indicate *up, down, forward, backward, left, right,* and so forth.

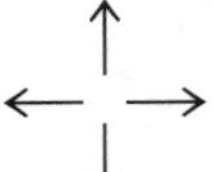

Suggestions	Add	Something like this
Enough/not enough		
Might be better/worse		
New position		
Forward/backward		
Left/right		
Up/down		
More/less		
Under/above		
When can I get a new seat/ seat cushion?		
How much will it cost overall?		
How much will it cost me?		
Who will fund this?		
When am I entitled to a new wheelchair?		
Can I get my wheelchair serviced in my home?		
Who should I call for wheelchair repairs?		
How long will it take to make the repairs?		
How long will it take to get a new wheelchair?		
When is my next appointment?		
Who should I call?		
What do you advise?		
Other:		

TIPS

Remember to give your seating clinician instructions as to how you want him or her to communicate with you.

Prepare phrases for meeting people or for giving a short "refresher" for people who know you but might have forgotten your communication style (see page 104 for more information).

Samples include the following:

- I say "yes" by nodding.
- I say "no" by shaking my head.
- I will hit my tray when I want to communicate something. Then I will point to the symbols on my tray.
- Please read aloud the word that is above the symbol that I point to with my left index finger.
- It is important for me to be involved in all decision making. Please let me know what is happening and ask for my input.

6

Transportation

People who use voice output devices for alternative and augmentative communication (AAC) may find the following words and phrases useful in booking transportation over the telephone. See Chapter 13, "Using the Telephone," for tips on communicating over the telephone.

AAC users who communicate with displays may need a translator or interpreter to make telephone calls to book transportation on their behalf. Again, see Chapter 13 for more information about utilizing translators for your telephone calls.

Some of the vocabulary in this chapter comes from a 1996 study conducted by Myers, Gibbons, Fried-Oken, and Bersani (see References and Vocabulary Resources). Other words and phrases come from The Aphasia Centre–North York, Ontario, Canada (see Appendix B).

Transportation

Suggestions	Add	Something like this
General Terms and Phrases		
I'd like to book a ride to		
My registration number is		
Could you book transportation for me?		
This is what I'd like you to say		
I'm in a power/manual wheelchair.		
Do you have to pick up other people?		
Can you send another bus/taxi?		
Please tell me what the dispatcher said.		
Did I miss my ride?		
My ride is late.		
Drop off		
Pick up		
What time can you pick me up?		
What is my pick up time?		
I want to cancel a booking.		
I need ______ days notice for transportation plans.		
Is it a bus or a taxi?		
I need a bus with a lift/ramp.		
I want to make a complaint.		
Safety		
Wheelchair accessibility		
Dispatcher		

TIPS

Dave uses an automatic telephone dial to book his routine transportation. His transportation booking script includes the following:

Hello. My name is Dave.

My registration number is ______.

I need to be picked up from (place) on (day) at (time).

I am traveling (alone/with someone).

I am going to ______.

I'd like a return pick up from there at ______. I will be going home.

Please repeat my booking to me.

That's correct.

That is wrong. Please wait while I correct that.

Thank you.

Suggestions	Add	Something like this
Get to places on time		
Driver's attitude		
Wait for the bus		
Give me time, please.		
Please be patient.		
I need more time.		
Please don't touch that.		
Bus passes		
Riding the bus		
Passenger's attitude		
I'm stuck.		
Help me push the wheelchair.		
Cost		
Catch the right bus		
Night service		
Citywide		
Statewide/provincewide		
Transportation		
City bus		
Subway		
Volunteer driver		
Taxi		
Train		
Airplane		
Ambulance		
Ticket		
Round-trip		
Schedule		

NOTES

7

Advocacy

If augmentative and alternative communication (AAC) users are to become effective advocates for their rights, they need to get involved in politics at the local and national levels. This chapter addresses vocabulary for politics and legislation, self-advocacy, and fund-raising. This vocabulary is particularly useful if you are a board member of an organization, task force, or committee. Some of the vocabulary in this chapter comes from a 1996 study conducted by Myers, Gibbons, Fried-Oken, and Bersani (see References and Vocabulary Resources).

Suggestions	Add	Something like this
Politics and Legislation		
Voting		
Making telephone calls		
Are you registered to vote?		
Will you support our issue?		
Do you have any family members with disabilities?		
I am a registered and active voter.		
How to contact		
Writing letters		
How to lobby		
Truth		
Call people in that office		
Get as much information as we need		
Do you feel strongly about disability issues?		
What will you do if elected?		
What will you do about the waiting list/need for services?		
What would you do if you were in my shoes?		
Do you know the candidates?		
What do they stand for?		
What is the law?		
Meeting		
Polling places		
Budget		

TIPS

Politics and Legislation

If necessary, customize this vocabulary to reflect the political terminology in your area, as well as your own political views and opinions.

You are encouraged to play an active role in advocating for your rights at local and national levels.

Some advocacy suggestions include:

- Get to know your local politicians.
- Prepare your issues beforehand.
- Mention that you vote, and state your concerns.
- Persevere with your issues.
- Join consumer organizations.

Suggestions	Add	Something like this
Barrier-free environment		
Committee hearing		
First/second/third reading		
Federal		
Provincial/statewide		
Taxation		
Politician		
Cabinet		
Governor/premier		
President/prime minister		
Congressperson		
Congressional district/ riding(s)		
Political party/parties		
Council		
Leader		
City bylaws		
Mayor		
Region(s)		
Zoning bylaws		
Parking regulations		
Prohibited grounds		
Introducing a bill		
Passing a bill		
Advocating/advocacy/ advocate		
Employment/unemployment		
Accommodation		
Outside sources of funding		

TIPS

How friends can help AAC users advocate for their rights:

- Be there.
- Ask politicians questions; demand that they give answers.
- Be part of the AAC user's life.
- Be informed; research what is needed.
- Involve the AAC user in every decision and process that affects him or her.
- Listen, support, and believe in the AAC user.

Advocacy

Suggestions	Add	Something like this
Undue hardship		
Lobbying		
Question period		
Speaker of the House of Representatives		
Elections		
City hall		
Townships		
Urban		
Rural		
Pollsters		
Citizenship		
Complaints		
Harassment		
Discrimination		
Freedom of information		
Privacy commission		
Campaign		
Official		
Administration		
Documents		
Strategic		
Health care		
Public hearing		
Other:		

TIPS

Roles that you can play as an AAC user:

- Know your rights.
- Speak out when your rights are violated.
- Ask others for help.
- Ask for information about the community, organizations, and policies.
- Build your confidence; believe in your future.

Suggestions	Add	Something like this
Self-Advocacy		
Take charge		
Freedom		
Resources		
Access		
Communication		
Mobility		
Skills		
Decision making		
Limitations		
Destiny		
Survive		
Support network		
The "real" world		
Goals		
Aspirations		
Options/no options		
Choice/lack of choice		
Control/lack of control		
Self-reliance		
Transition		
Secure/insecure		
Responsibility		
Getting the help I need		
I can do that myself.		
I need you to help me with		
Handle		
Exert control		

TIPS

Self-Advocacy

These words and phrases have to do with advocacy, opportunity, and breaking down barriers.

They were collected from conversations about empowerment among speaking people with disabilities.

Advocacy

Suggestions	Add	Something like this
Expand my options		
Help make decisions		
Fend for myself		
Everyday activities		
Empowerment		
Independence		
Other:		

TIPS

The International Society for Augmentative and Alternative Communication (ISAAC) is an organization of AAC users and their family members, researchers, and service providers. It aims to advance the field of AAC and to foster the exchange of knowledge. ISAAC is actively seeking more AAC users as members. Membership entails the ISAAC Bulletin, with Mike Joyce's thoughtful and entertaining Consumer Corner; reduced fees for publications and conferences; an opportunity to apply for scholarships and awards; participation in the consumer program at the Biennial conference; partial scholarships for attending the conference; and opportunities to develop leadership skills and serve on ISAAC committees. As a member of ISAAC, you have an opportunity to influence the AAC field, which has a great impact on people's lives.

To find out more, contact ISAAC:

International Society for
Augmentative and Alternative
Communication (ISAAC)
49 The Donway West
Suite 308
Toronto, Ontario
M3C 3M9
Canada
(416) 385-0351

Suggestions	Add	Something like this
Fund-Raising		
When does the fiscal year end?		
We need money.		
Cooperation		
Donations		
Maintaining the organization		
New ideas		
I learned that the hard way.		
How much money is left?		
I have an idea.		
Why do we need money?		
Who controls the money?		
How can we make money?		
What do you think about that?		
Advocacy		
Sponsorships		
Power for self-advocates to make decisions		
Around the state/province		
Bill		
What will it cost?		
Can we do that?		
Maintaining the budget		
Fund-raising		
Garage sales		
Concert/dance/social		
Raffle		
The bank		

TIPS

Fund-Raising

More and more AAC users are being asked to get involved in committees and task forces to advocate for the rights of people with disabilities.

There are many opportunities for you to get involved. If you are on a committee, it is likely that much of your time will be spent discussing money and fund-raising initiatives. Many of these words and phrases might be useful when discussing fund-raising.

See other sections in this chapter:

- Politics and Legislation
- Self-Advocacy

Also see Chapter 8, "Banking and Finances."

8

Banking and Finances

Looking after one's own finances and doing one's own banking can be a challenge for some augmentative and alternative communication (AAC) users. The right words and phrases are needed to discuss money. This chapter provides such vocabulary, as well as vocabulary and tips for preparing tax returns.

You may also need some help in learning how to manage your finances. Most independent living or transition programs provide assistance and training in this area. Contact your local service agency for more information on this matter.

Banking and Finances

Suggestions	Add	Something like this
General Terms and Phrases		
What's my balance?		
I need a withdrawal slip.		
I need a deposit slip.		
I'd like to pay my phone bill.		
I'd like to cash this check.		
I want to deposit this into my checking account savings account money market account individual retirement account (IRA)/retirement savings plan		
I need some help with my ATM card.		
I would like to transfer money from one account to another.		
Check/checkbook		
Change/coins		
Bankbook/passbook		
I'd like to borrow money.		
Cash		
Statement		
Deposit/deposit slip		
Withdrawal/withdrawal slip		
Bank card		
Bank machine/ATM		
Loan		

TIPS

For more vocabulary about money, see the fund-raising section of "Advocacy" (Chapter 7).

Suggestions	Add	Something like this
Credit card		
MasterCard		
Visa		
American Express		
Discover		
Home ownership		
Investment(s)		
Payment		
Numbers		
Rent/mortgage		
Budget		
Monthly income		
Gross/net		
Monthly expenditures		
Update		
Interest		
Daily/monthly/annually		
Preauthorization		
Calculator with large buttons		
Traveler's checks		
Receipt		
Money order		
Signature		
Direct payment		
Trace		
Stop payment		
Charges		
Teller		
Bank manager		

TIPS

In addition to this suggested vocabulary, you will need money words (e.g., *dollar, cent, dime, nickel*) and numbers.

It is a good idea to prepare your messages before you go to the bank. If you have an AAC device, you can program your messages ahead of time. You might also consider printing out a message on your computer and taking that message to the bank teller.

Banking and Finances

Suggestions	Add	Something like this
Loan officer		
Credit rating		
Safety deposit box		
Power of attorney		
Identification		
Change of address		
Telephone number		
Mutual funds		
Bonds		
Foreign market		
Witness		
Disability insurance		
Financial advisor		
Welfare		
Tax credit		
Social Security		
Eligible/ineligible		
Medical expenses		
Renovations		
Income		
Taxable benefits		
Tax form/tax guide		
Attendant care expense form		
Family benefits		
Social assistance/welfare		
Worker's compensation		
Other:		

TIPS

Some AAC users suggest getting to know one or two tellers well so they can become familiar with your style of communication.

Depending on where you live, alternate formats for tax information may be available. These may include audiotapes, large-print forms, and computer disks. Check with your local taxation office regarding this matter.

9

Grocery Shopping

Many augmentative and alternative communication (AAC) users can shop independently in supermarkets. They can select what they want and may only need to communicate with the cashier. It is often necessary, however, to take someone along with you who can reach for items or to have that person shop for you. Having someone shop with or for you means you need vocabulary that applies to regular grocery shopping.

No attempt was made to list everything available at a grocery store. Instead, this chapter simply includes phrases and words that some AAC users find helpful. Remember, therefore, to add any words that you need to your personal vocabulary list.

Grocery Shopping

Suggestions	Add	Something like this
General Terms and Phrases		
How much is it?		
Which do you think I should get?		
I need help, please.		
Is it on sale?		
What's on sale?		
May I have a sale flier?		
Can I return this?		
It's not right.		
I would like to exchange this.		
May I have a refund, please?		
Please follow me.		
Let me show you what I mean.		
I'm just looking around.		
Could you please give me change for this?		
This doesn't work.		
Thank you for your assistance.		
Can you help me get something?		
I'll point to it.		
Say the name of each item in the area in which I am pointing. I'll let you know when you say the name of the one I want.		

TIPS

Jim, an AAC user, suggests that you prepare your grocery list ahead of time. He keeps his list in a computer file, as he tends to buy or replace similar items. He can then edit this list every week. He either takes the list to his local grocery store or asks his personal assistant to do the shopping for him.

Suggestions	Add	Something like this
Can you help me reach this, please?		
Do you accept credit cards?		
Which credit cards do you accept?		
May I have a paper/plastic bag?		
Please put my groceries in the bag behind my wheelchair/on my lap.		
Could you weigh this, please?		
Please get the money out of my wallet and count it in front of me.		
Other:		

TIPS

Include quantity words, such as numbers, weights, *more, less,* and so forth.

10

Eating Out

Michael Williams, a user of augmentative and alternative communication (AAC), is the editor of a publication called *Alternatively Speaking* (see Appendix B for more information). He wrote in his 1994 article "How Do You Say *Hamburger*?" about his experience of going out to eat. He said he always worries about the following: how accessible the restaurant is, whether the server will understand how he communicates, whether the server will give him the time he needs to communicate his order, whether he will have to deal with the server's embarrassment in the event that he or she cannot understand Williams's communication, and whether he will need to spend time trying to make himself understood.

This chapter suggests vocabulary from which you can chose so you can be prepared for some of the situations that Williams identified. It includes words and phrases for ordering a meal at a restaurant and inquiring about a restaurant's degree of accessibility.

Eating Out

Suggestions	Add	Something like this
Ordering		
Please read these items aloud, and I will tell you when you say the name of the one I want.		
Please read the menu aloud.		
What are today's specials?		
May I see the menu, please?		
I'd like the		
Is this kosher?		
I'm a vegetarian.		
Please put that on the side.		
Please cut the food.		
What is your house wine?		
What beers do you have?		
What vegetables do you have?		
What desserts do you have?		
Could you tell me what's in it?		
Does this contain any meat or animal products?		
How is it cooked/prepared?		
I'm allergic to		
What will you have?		
Which credit cards do you accept?		
How much is it?		
May I have the bill, please?		
Tip		

TIPS

Michael Williams (1994) suggests that you have an introduction card ready when you go out to a restaurant, even if you use a voice output device (see Chapter 12, "Social Conversations," for more information). If you use a device, make sure it is set up for the best possible speech output.

Suggestions	Add	Something like this
Descriptions for Food		
Delicious		
Strong		
Terrible		
Tasty		
Sour		
Sweet		
Salty		
Spicy		
Bitter		
Bland		
Burned		
Good		
Greasy		
Underdone		
Other:		

TIPS

It is a good idea to include on your list the types of ethnic restaurants at which you may want to eat (e.g., Italian, Chinese).

Suggestions	Add	Something like this
Utensils		
Fork/knife/spoon		
Napkins		
Plate/bowl/saucer		
Cup/mug/glass		
Flexible straw		
Nonslip mat		
Clothing protector		
Accessibility		
Ramp		
Level entrance		
Elevator		
Automatic doors		
Designated parking		
Self-serve area		
I don't want a booth.		
Is there enough space for my wheelchair at a table?		
Is there a wheelchair-accessible bathroom?		
Please remove the chairs from around the table.		
I want to be seated near/not near the speakers.		
I want to be seated in the smoking/nonsmoking section.		
Is your building wheelchair accessible?		
Stairs/steps		
I'd like to be seated where there's good lighting.		

TIPS

Bruce always asks to sit in a well-lit area when he goes to a restaurant. This is important, as he needs to see and point to items on his communication display.

11

Requesting Clarification

This chapter suggests vocabulary for telling your conversation partner that you have a problem understanding what he or she is saying and telling your partner how he or she can help you understand. The phrases in this chapter are especially handy to have near you when you are learning a new task (e.g., when being shown how to operate a software program on your computer or how to program your communication device). Nonetheless, it is often difficult to remember everything when learning a new task. You should feel comfortable asking your tutor or clinician to write down or videotape instructions to which you can refer when you need the information.

Requesting Clarification

Suggestions	Add	Something like this
Communicating that You Have a Problem		
Excuse me!		
I need help.		
I'd like some assistance.		
Could you please help me?		
What do you mean?		
I don't understand.		
I don't understand the terminology.		
I'm not sure about that.		
I don't get it.		
I don't know what you mean.		
You're losing me.		
Other:		

TIPS

Never be afraid to ask your doctor, clinician, teacher, or service provider to slow down, to say things again, or to use everyday language.

Select a few phrases from this list to keep beside you when you are involved in educational sessions or health care consultation.

Suggestions	Add	Something like this
Communicating How You Want Help		
Please explain.		
Please repeat that.		
Go a bit slower/faster.		
Write it down for me.		
Please speak up.		
Record your instructions on an audiotape.		
Can you videotape this so I can look at it later?		
Please type the instructions into my device so I can listen to them later.		
Please go over that again.		
Please let me try it.		
Watch and tell me if I am doing it correctly.		
I understand.		
Show me.		
I want to make sure I understand.		
Can I call you if I have a problem?		
I need some time to think about it.		
Can we stop now?		
I feel a bit overwhelmed right now.		
Other:		

NOTES

12

Social Conversations

Successful communication depends on two or more people giving and receiving messages from each other. This means that in addition to your knowing how to use your augmentative and alternative communication (AAC) system, your speaking partners must also know how you communicate and what they can do to make communication successful.

In their 1998 book *Building Communicative Competence with Individuals Who Use Augmentative and Alternative Communication,* Light and Binger reported that AAC users who explain how they communicate are more likely to have successful interactions when meeting new people. Light and Binger's book gives step-by-step procedures to help AAC users develop introductions and learn to use them.

This chapter provides sample vocabulary that you may want to use in the following situations:

- Explaining to someone how you communicate
- Telling someone what they should do when communicating with you
- Using greetings
- Engaging in small talk
- Meeting new people
- Delivering quick responses
- Using wrap-ups and farewells

Suggestions	Add	Something like this
How You Communicate		
Hi, my name is		
Please read this. It will help us communicate.		
I can hear and understand everything that you say.		
I have difficulty speaking, so I use this machine/display to communicate.		
I have trouble using my muscles; that's why I can't speak.		
I communicate "yes" by ____ and "no" by ____.		
This is a talking machine. I program it with the words I need.		
I point to the words/pictures on this display that I want to communicate.		
I use my ______ finger on my ______ hand to point.		
I use sign language to communicate. Let me know if you don't understand my signs. I'll use this book to show you what I am saying.		
I spell out what I want to say on this display/device.		
I use my eyes to communicate. Read the instructions and look at the photographs to see how I communicate with my eyes.		

TIPS

Meeting People

Williams said that a card that tells people you have difficulty speaking and that you communicate by pointing to words (or pictures or letters) or use a device to communicate can "work wonders when you spring an AAC system on someone for the first time . . . It really puts people in a listening mood. Try it, you may be amazed by the results" (1994, p. 5).

Your card should give short and easy instructions on how you communicate and what your partner can do to make communication successful.

Many AAC users put their introductions on the front page of their AAC displays or program them into their devices.

Your introduction does not have to give your name, nor does it have to give your medical diagnosis (unless you want to include them).

Suggestions	Add	Something like this
What Your Partner Should Do		
Read the word aloud so I know that you understand my message.		
Let me know if you don't understand what I am saying.		
Please talk to me like an adult.		
Please give me a lot of time.		
Write down the message as I spell it/compose it.		
If you know the word I am spelling, you can guess it.		
Please wait until I am finished my message before guessing what I mean.		
Please hold my display in front of me.		
You can read the screen if you don't understand.		
Please stand on my ______ side.		
Stand in front of me when you are speaking with me.		
Sometimes I jumble my words. If this happens, let me finish, and then guess what I mean.		
Other:		

TIPS

Light and Binger (1998) stated that the AAC user's asking questions about the other person enhances interactions between AAC users and adult conversation partners. As people love to talk about themselves, this technique actually works to put new or unfamiliar partners at ease when they first meet an AAC user.

Pat's introduction follows:

- Hi, I'm Pat.
- I say "ya" for *yes* and "uh-uh" for *no*.
- I use sign language to communicate.
- Let me know if you do not understand my signs, and I'll point to the picture of what I am communicating about.
- Just read the word that appears above the picture.
- Thanks.

Suggestions	Add	Something like this
Greetings		
Hi, how's it going?		
Hello.		
How are you?		
Nice to meet you.		
Nice to see you again.		
Long time, no see.		
What have you been up to?		
Good morning/evening.		
What's new?		
What's happening?		
What's up?		
Other:		

TIPS

These phrases are only suggestions. You should develop phrases for greeting, engaging in chitchat, and so forth that reflect your personality and interests.

Suggestions	Add	Something like this
Small Talk		
It's hot these days!		
Boy, it's cold!		
When will this weather clear up?		
When will summer come?		
What about those (name of sports team)?		
Have you seen any good movies recently?		
How's your family?		
How was your vacation?		
How was your weekend?		
Any plans for the weekend?		
Did you know that		
What about you?		
What do you think?		
Do you agree?		
What are your views on this?		
What music are you into these days?		
I really enjoyed that movie. How about you?		
So, what did you think of the Academy Awards?		
Other:		

TIPS

Prepare questions and opinions about current events in your device. If you use a display, have a page set aside for current topics and issues. Arrange for someone to assist you in selecting items and cutting out text and pictures from newspapers or magazines.

Suggestions	Add	Something like this
Meeting New People		
I'm from ______. Have you ever been there?		
Where are you from?		
What are your interests?		
Where do you work?		
Where do you go to school?		
Where do you live?		
Tell me about your family.		
What sports do you follow?		
What music do you like?		
I'm into computers. How about you?		
Do you know		
Other:		

TIPS

Much of conversation is storytelling. When you are designing your display or programming your device, you may want to structure your stories so you can control the timing of delivery. This way, you can give your partner opportunities to comment and respond. You might also include the following elements in your storytelling:

1. Setting
   (who the story is about, when and where the story happened)
2. Issue or predicament
   (the "meat" of the story)
3. Response (from other people and you)
4. Outcome (what actually happened at the end of the story)

Suggestions	Add	Something like this
Quick Responses		
Yeah.		
Sure.		
Good.		
Cool!		
Great!		
Way to go!		
That's a blast!		
Interesting.		
That's funny/wild.		
Really?		
I don't believe it.		
You don't say?		
Too bad.		
Gross!		
That's a pity.		
Sorry to hear that.		
You're pulling my leg!		
No way!		
You're joking!		
Excuse me.		
What?		
When?		
Where?		
Why?		
Why not?		
Who?		
How?		

TIPS

Reflect your age, personality, and culture in your quick responses. Slang words and phrases work well here.

Suggestions	Add	Something like this
Wrap-Ups		
Well, I have to be off now.		
Good chatting with you.		
I'm in a bit of a hurry. Can we catch up later?		
Say "hi" to everyone for me.		
I'll be in touch.		
Give me a call sometime.		
We should get together soon.		
I'm late for an appointment.		
Got to go.		
Farewells		
Good-bye.		
So long.		
Bye for now.		
See you soon.		
Have a good day/evening.		
Catch up with you later.		
Great seeing you.		

TIPS

Wrap-ups are used to tell the person with whom you are communicating that you are about to say good-bye and leave. People who speak subtly convey this message in a variety of different ways (e.g., body language, intonation) before actually saying good-bye. AAC users who cannot use these signals may want to select and use a number of wrap-up phrases prior to a farewell.

13

Using the Telephone

Telecommunications play an increasingly significant role in social contact, recreation, education, and employment. The telephone can be a major problem for many people who use augmentative and alternative communication (AAC). As of the end of the 20th century, however, there are many different ways to keep in touch with people. You may want to explore using fax machines or e-mail in addition to the telephone. If you are interested in these options, contact your local AAC service.

This chapter provides vocabulary and tips for using a voice output communication aid (VOCA) when calling someone on the telephone whom you do not know, making quick responses, and using clarification techniques when you are not understood. Vocabulary and tips are also presented for asking someone to make a call on your behalf, using a translator (i.e., someone who repeats everything you communicate), and using an interpreter (i.e., someone who interprets what you want to communicate).

Suggestions	Add	Something like this
Calling Someone You Do Not Know This is _______. I have a speech problem. I use a machine to talk. Hello, please don't hang up. This is _______. I have difficulty speaking, so I am using a device to talk to you. Can you understand me? Please wait while I prepare a message. It takes a little while, so please be patient. If you ask me yes/no questions, I can respond more quickly. Call me back when it's a good time to chat. This is _______. Could you please call me back? My telephone number is _______. May I speak with Hi, this is _______. I'd like to speak with _______. Other:		

TIPS

Handling the Telephone

It is best to use a hands-free telephone or speakerphone in conjunction with a voice output device. Many new telephones come with this feature.

You may be able to get a catalog of different types of telephones from your local telephone center.

Manufacturers and vendors of assistive devices may also have a range of adaptive telephones.

Some countries/areas offer cost reductions for the rental of telephones and long-distance telephone calls for people with speech disorders. They may also have relay services, which some AAC users find useful. Contact your local office about these matters.

Answering the Telephone

Sue uses an answering machine to screen her telephone calls. If the caller is someone she knows, she will answer it. Familiar callers know to stay on the line to give Sue the time she needs to get to the telephone. Sue prefers to return calls to unfamiliar callers, as this gives her time to position her voice output device close to the telephone and/or to arrange for a translator to assist with her communication.

Suggestions	Add	Something like this
Quick Responses		
Yes.		
No.		
Maybe.		
Sure.		
Good.		
That's too bad.		
I don't think so.		
I know.		
I don't know.		
I'm not sure.		
I understand.		
I don't understand.		
That's not what I meant to say.		
Please say that again.		
I can't hear you.		
I have something to say about that. Please give me a minute to compose my message.		
Thank you.		
Talk to you later.		
Good-bye.		
Other:		

TIPS

Using a Voice Output Device Over the Telephone

1. Position the telephone speaker so you can hear what your partner is saying to you and he or she can hear what you are communicating through your device.
2. Speed is a problem when communicating on the telephone. Silence is not tolerated, particularly at the beginning of a conversation. People will hang up! You need to have frequently used phrases already programmed in your device.
3. Have an introductory message ready for new listeners.
4. If you have a specific message, you can program this ahead of time.
5. Don't use long sentences all at once. Listeners who are not used to hearing communication devices may take longer to understand what you are saying. Break your sentence into three- to four-word chunks or phrases and give your listener time to process what you are saying. This will also give the listener a chance to tell you if he or she does not understand.

(*continued on p. 114*)

Suggestions	Add	Something like this
Clarifications		
Please let me know if you cannot understand what I am saying.		
I will spell that for you.		
It might help if you write down what I am saying.		
That's not what I meant.		
Is there anyone else there who could help me?		
Let's start again.		
Please tell me what you understand so far.		
I'm going to spell out what I am saying.		
Do you understand me?		
Please say that again.		
I'm having trouble hearing you.		
Can I call you back?		
I can't talk about that right now.		
I'm going to spell that: *A* as in *apple* *B* as in *baby* *C* as in *Charlie* *D* as in *David*		
Other:		

TIPS

6. If the listener does not understand you, try
   - Asking him or her to repeat back what he or she understands so far
   - Informing the listener that you will spell the word letter by letter
   - Giving a word clue for letters, such as "A as in apple" if the listener has trouble understanding a letter (you need to program your device ahead of time to use this approach)
7. Sometimes even the best voice output devices can be difficult to understand over the telephone. For important calls, you might want to have an interpreter or translator available in case you run into difficulties. (See the section in this chapter about using interpreters.)

Suggestions	Add	Something like this
Asking Someone to Make a Call on Your Behalf		
Would you make a telephone call for me?		
I want you to call		
Please tell him/her that you are calling on my behalf.		
Give him/her this message.		
Please do not answer questions or give any more information.		
Please tell me what he/she said.		
I want you to find out some information for me.		
Please negotiate this for me and let me know.		
Please check with me before giving an answer.		
Other:		

TIPS

AAC users say that they want their attendants to do one of the following:

- Deliver a message on the AAC user's behalf
- Negotiate on the AAC user's behalf
- Translate or interpret over the telephone.

If you require telephone assistance, be sure to give clear instructions to the person helping you.

Using the Telephone

Suggestions	Add	Something like this
Instructions for a Translator		
Please use a speakerphone so I can hear what the person is saying.		
Please sit close to the telephone so the person can hear what you say as I point to the items on my display.		
Please say this when you make the call: "My name is (first name). I am acting as a translator for ______. He/she has a speech disorder. We are using a speakerphone so he/she can hear what you are saying. My role is to tell you the words/letters to which he/she is pointing OR help out only if you have trouble understanding what he/she is saying. Please let me know if you cannot understand.		
You may proceed with your conversation with______.		
Please just read aloud the words to which I point. Do not add any new information.		
Tell the person on the telephone that it may take a minute for me to compose my response.		
Tell the person on the telephone that you need to check with me.		

TIPS

Some AAC users employ a translator for making telephone calls. It is important to establish that the telephone call is between the AAC user and the person on the other end of the telephone. To do this Krezman and Williams (1991) suggest the following:

- The translator should introduce the conversation by saying something such as "My name is (first name only). I am acting as a translator for ______. He has a speech disorder, and I am here in case you have difficulty understanding his communication."
- If using a standard telephone, the translator tells the caller, "Please wait until I find out how ______ wants to respond" and relays what the other person has said to the AAC user. This action gives proof to the caller that the message is being relayed to you and that you are in control of the conversation.

Suggestions	Add	Something like this
Instructions for an Interpreter		
(In addition to phrases for a translator)		
Please tell the person on the telephone to wait while you find out what I want to communicate.		
Please guess what I mean. Please check with me first and then when I am sure you know what I want to say, tell the person on the telephone.		
Before you dial, I want to tell you what we will be communicating about.		
Please put my words into a sentence.		
Other:		

TIPS

A translator's role is to repeat everything that the AAC user wants to communicate in the exact way the AAC user communicated it. A translator does not add any interpretation or comments.

An interpreter's role is to repeat everything the AAC user communicates and, if necessary, interpret what the AAC user is communicating, get confirmation on this from the AAC user, and convey the intended message to the person on the telephone. AAC users who do not communicate in full sentences or may not have the vocabulary they need to communicate what they want may require an interpreter.

14

Safety

This chapter provides suggested vocabulary for security issues and emergencies. Whether you live in a house, apartment complex, or group home, you can reduce your vulnerability to crime and other emergency situations by practicing good safety and security habits. Find out about safety training and crime prevention programs in your area for people with disabilities. In addition, ask for advice on how safety systems and procedures can be adapted for or utilized by an augmentative and alternative communication (AAC) user.

Safety

Suggestions	Add	Something like this
Security Issues		
Safe/unsafe		
Hurt/harm		
Suspicious		
Wary		
Bothering		
Familiar/unfamiliar person		
Stranger		
Suspicious person		
Insecure		
Security guard		
Security system		
Alarm		
Personal safety device		
Telephone		
Smoke detector/CO_2 detector		
Batteries		
Keys		
Deadbolt/chain		
Pull the blinds		
Leave on the light/radio		
Buzzer/peephole/door opener		
Intercom/identify		
Well-lit/dark		
Places: park street workplace		

TIPS

Emergency Information

If you use a communication device, it is a good idea to program some emergency phrases for use over the telephone or in face-to-face interactions. If you use a display, you can set aside a section for this information or transcribe it on a small card taped to the inside of your armrest.

Keep the information to a minimum. In an emergency, people do not have the time to read long instructions.

Your card may contain

- Your name
- Contact person in case of emergency
- How you say "yes" and "no"
- How you use your display/device
- A statement that you should be consulted on all major decisions regarding your care
- Medical emergency information (e.g., allergies)

Suggestions	Add	Something like this
home laundry room washroom bus bar restaurant back alley elevator		
Day/night		
People around		
Emergency		
Call for help		
Hide		
Trapped		
Locked/unlocked		
Open/closed		
Police check/check references		
Report/disclose		
Emergency numbers: 911 (fire department/ police) doctor neighbor poison control center		
Professional assistance service		
Safe-deposit box		
Cash/valuables		
Street-smart		
Take precautions		
Other:		

TIPS

Out of Harm's Way: A Safety Kit for People with Disabilities Who Feel Unsafe and Want to Do Something About It (1997) is available from the Roeher Institute:
Roeher Institute
York University
Kinsmen Building
4700 Keele Street
North York, Ontario
M3J 1P3
Canada

Suggestions	Add	Something like this
Emergencies		
Call 911		
Please send an ambulance to		
This is ______. I have a disability.		
Please call		
My name is ______. I live at ______.		
I need help.		
I repeat, this is an emergency.		
I'm in trouble.		
Please help me.		
I need you to help me with		
Ambulance		
Paramedics		
Police		
Accident		
Medic-alert bracelet		
Hospital		
Poison control center		
Injury		
Crisis center		
Break-in		
Smell of gas		
Explosion		
Crime		
Doctor		
Emergency room		
Nurse		

TIPS

The text on Aaron's card for hospital emergencies follows:

My name is Aaron. I have cerebral palsy. I hear and understand everything. The person who is with me is helping me, but I need to know what is going on. I will make my own decisions. Please explain everything you are doing, and ask me for my consent. Ask me where the pain is by naming each body part. I'll indicate *yes* by lifting my eyes when you name the one where I feel pain. Ask me "Is it a dull pain? Is it a sharp pain?" Ask me to describe the pain's severity on a scale of 1 to 5: 1 is mild pain; 5 is intense pain. Start counting slowly. I'll lift my eyes when you say the number I want.

Suggestions	Add	Something like this
Staff		
Walk-in clinic		
Family member		
Cardiopulmonary resuscitation (CPR)		
First aid		
I'm allergic to		
Please read about how I communicate in the binder that is in my bag.		
Other:		

TIPS

Jeff keeps a binder in the bag behind his wheelchair. In this binder, he has documented instructions on how people can assist him in the following areas:

- How to communicate with him
- How to lift him
- How to help him eat and drink
- How to take off his coat
- How to assist him in the washroom

He has a separate section about helping him in an emergency situation.

15

Participating at a Convention

People who use augmentative and alternative communication (AAC) are attending more conventions, not only to learn about the options available to them but also to contribute and to provide valuable input to other AAC users, service providers, researchers, and manufacturers of communication systems and devices.

Although there are many pertinent conventions, the following are particularly exciting for AAC users (see Appendix B for more information):

- ISAAC (International Society for Augmentative and Alternative Communication)
- PEC (Pittsburgh Employment Conference for Augmented Communicators)
- CAMA (Communication Aids Manufacturers Association)

The following lists provide words and phrases for participating at AAC conventions. Some of the vocabulary in this chapter comes from a 1996 study conducted by Myers, Gibbons, Fried-Oken, and Bersani (see References and Vocabulary Resources).

Participating at a Convention

Suggestions	Add	Something like this
General Terms and Phrases		
How much will it cost?		
Set up a committee		
Let's meet every month.		
Workshops		
Support is necessary		
Wear nice clothes		
Be on time		
Friends		
Power to self-advocates		
Excuse me, I have something to say.		
Aye (for voting)		
Nay—I object (for voting)		
Please don't treat me like that.		
Who runs the convention?		
Get the committee members.		
Planning		
Access to hotels		
Travel		
Officers		
Understand each other		
Let's work, not just play.		
I need help.		
This place is not wheelchair accessible.		
Is there a theme?		
This group has good staff/ members.		

TIPS

The tips for oral speakers and AAC users on the next two pages are from Fried-Oken, Creech, and Baker (1994). They were developed specifically for the 1994 Biennial Conference of the International Society for Augmentative and Alternative Communication. You may want to share these tips with other people.

Each participant should

- Treat everyone with respect
- Listen to whomever is speaking
- Take the time needed to say what he or she wants to say

Suggestions	Add	Something like this
People with different jobs		
Money		
Banquet		
Meetings		
I have a comment on this topic.		
Please let me come back to it later.		
Wait a minute.		
I will respond to that in a moment.		
I am composing something that I need to say now.		
I have a question.		
I don't understand what you're saying.		
I want to refer to something you said a few moments ago. The topic was		
I'm talking. Please don't interrupt me.		
I haven't finished. Let me continue.		
I'd like to say something about that.		
Excuse me.		
Please take notes for me.		
May I have a copy of the handouts?		
Other:		

TIPS

For Oral Speakers

Do not speak for an AAC user unless invited by the AAC user to do so.

Ask for clarification or repetition if you do not understand what an AAC user has said.

If the AAC user's communication is not understood by the presenter, the AAC user should get a couple of chances to make himself or herself understood.

The audience should not chime in to clarify interactions between an AAC user and a speaker unless invited to do so.

It is not polite to pretend that you have understood an AAC user when you have not. Requests for clarification are generally not offensive to AAC users.

Participating at a Convention

Suggestions	Add	Something like this
May I audiotape the discussion?		
Turn on/off my tape recorder.		
I'd like to comment on that after the break.		
Please speak up.		
Repeat the question.		
I can/can't see.		
I want to sit closer/farther back.		
When is the break?		
Will there be time for questions?		
Other:		

TIPS

For AAC Users

AAC users need a way to signal that they have something to say. Develop ways to interrupt presenters politely. If it will take 2–3 minutes to generate a comment, it is suggested that you compose your message in private and then speak it publicly on your device.

In order to change a topic, identify the topic first.

During public presentations, consider turning off access feedback (beeps and tones) during the message preparation unless feedback is necessary.

Check your volume before the speaker starts.

Consider customizing a standard voice so you can be identified in a group setting. Consider repeating the whole sentence after presenting a comment word by word. Preprogram some of the sentences suggested in this chapter.

16

Sexuality

According to Farrar,

> Sexuality is more than sex. Our sexuality is everything that makes us female or male. We are female and male because of our bodies. We are female or male because of our feelings. We are female or male because of our minds and because of our relationships with other people. Sexuality is a big part of living for all of us. (1996, p. 21)

The vocabulary in this chapter has been compiled to reflect words required for describing pleasurable sexual experiences as well as sexual abuse. It suggests vocabulary for body parts, reproduction and health, relationships, feelings and descriptions, and sexual activity. Access to this vocabulary allows augmentative and alternative communication (AAC) users to communicate about, question, and understand healthy sexuality. Knowing about healthy sexuality and the boundaries of privacy helps AAC users recognize and protect themselves from sexual abuse.

Sexuality

Suggestions	Add	Something like this
Body		
Male/female		
Genitals/private parts		
Pubic hair		
Vulva		
Labia		
Urethra		
Uterus		
Fallopian tube(s)		
Ovaries		
Vagina		
Clitoris		
Breast(s)		
Penis		
Foreskin		
Scrotum		
Testicles/balls		
Vas deferens		
Semen		
Sperm		
Hand(s)		
Finger(s)		
Mouth		
Tongue		
Anus		
Bottom/buttocks/bum		
Other:		

TIPS

Farrar's (1996) *End the Silence: Preventing the Sexual Assault of Women with Communication Disabilities: Developing a Community Response* is an excellent resource manual for women who use AAC and their service providers. It contains a comprehensive list of resources.

For more information, contact:

Technical Resource Centre
200, 1201-5 Street SW
Calgary, Alberta
T2R 0Y6
Canada
(403) 262-9445

Suggestions	Add	Something like this
Reproduction and Health		
Abortion		
Acquired immunodeficiency syndrome (AIDS)		
Birth		
Birth control		
Cervical cap		
Chlamydia		
Condom		
Conception		
Contraception		
Cramps		
Diaphragm		
Dry		
Egg		
Ejaculation		
Erection		
Family planning		
Female condom		
Fertility tester		
Fertilization		
Genital warts		
Gonorrhea		
Hepatitis B		
Herpes		
Human immunodeficiency virus (HIV)		
Hurt		
Hysterectomy		

TIPS

According to the International Planned Parenthood Federation (Farrar, 1996), when you visit the doctor, you have the right to

- Receive accessible health services
- Be treated with dignity and respect no matter what your age, race, sexual orientation, physical or mental abilities, or economic status
- Explain how your belongings and adaptive devices are handled during the visit
- Have your records kept private and confidential
- Be given explanations and answers to your questions
- Receive education and counseling about medical concerns
- Be interviewed and examined in a private room
- Bring a friend to assist you in your visit
- Know the names of the people serving you
- Agree to or refuse any care or treatment

Suggestions	Add	Something like this
Implant		
Infection		
Injection		
Intercourse		
Intrauterine device (IUD)		
Menstruation		
Natural birth control		
Pain		
Pap smear		
Pelvic exam		
Period		
Pill		
Pregnant		
Premenstrual syndrome (PMS)		
Prescription		
Pubic lice/crabs		
Reproduction		
Safe sex		
Sexually transmitted disease		
Spermicidal jelly		
Sterilization		
Syphilis		
Tubal ligation		
Vaginal contraceptive sponge		
Vaginal spermicide		
Vasectomy		

TIPS

According to the International Planned Parenthood Federation (Farrar, 1996), when you visit a doctor, you also have the right to

- Review your medical records with your doctor
- Agree to or refuse to have an observer present during the examination or interview
- Ask for a particular doctor or nurse when scheduling your appointment
- Express your opinion about the services you received

Suggestions	Add	Something like this
Relationships		
Abuse		
Affection		
Bad		
Bisexual		
Boyfriend		
Break up		
Celibate		
Close		
"Coming out"		
Commitment		
Consenting		
Couple		
Courting		
Date/dating		
Engagement		
Falling in love/out of love		
Fondness		
Friendship		
Gay		
Girlfriend		
Going out/going steady		
Good		
Harassment		
Heterosexual		
Homophobia		
Homosexual		
Intimate		

NOTES

Sexuality

Suggestions	Add	Something like this
"Just friends"		
Lesbian		
Lover(s)		
Loving		
Marriage		
Privacy/no privacy		
Relationship		
Romance/romantic		
Safe		
Sexual orientation		
Straight		
Supportive		
Sweethearts		
Transsexual		
Other:		

TIPS

Lindsey and Millin remarked:

> We consider our sexuality as probably the most private part of ourselves, the most difficult to disclose. In spite of our discomfort, talk we must. We must provide those who cannot speak appropriate opportunities to learn about their own sexuality and needs for intimacy. It must be dignified and respected but it must be done. (1998, p. 2)

Suggestions	Add	Something like this
Feelings/Descriptions		
(Include *not, very,* and *a little*)		
Afraid		
Aggressive		
Angry		
Anxious		
Ashamed		
Attractive		
Bad		
Beautiful		
Better		
Brave		
Careful		
Cautious		
Cheap		
Clean		
Cold		
Comfortable		
Concerned		
Considerate		
Cooperative		
Cranky		
Cruel		
Delighted		
Depressed		
Difficult		
Dirty		
Disappointed		

TIPS

Farrar stated:

> People who use AAC often must rely on others to include vocabulary about sexuality on their displays or devices. This vocabulary is often omitted. Without it, education in and discussion of personal safety, healthy sexuality and sexual assault cannot occur. (on a promotional flier)

Sexuality

Suggestions	Add	Something like this
Disgusted		
Embarrassed		
Emotional		
Enjoyable		
Enthusiastic		
Envious		
Erotic		
Excellent		
Excited		
Exhausted		
Fair		
Foolish		
Forgiving		
Frantic		
Frustrated		
Generous		
Gentle		
Grateful		
Greedy		
Guilty		
Helpless		
Honest		
Horny		
Humiliated		
Hurt		
Ignored		
Impatient		
Important		
Interested		

TIPS

Farrar asserted:

> Everyone has the right to accurate information about human growth and development, human reproduction, anatomy, physiology, masturbation, pregnancy, childbirth, parenthood, family life, sexual response, sexual orientation, contraception, abortion, sexual abuse, HIV/AIDS and other sexually transmitted diseases, and preventive sexual and reproductive health. (on a promotional flier)

Feelings/Descriptions

Suggestions	Add	Something like this
Intimate		
Intrigued		
Irritated		
Jealous		
Kind		
Kinky		
Left out		
Lonely		
Loving		
Macho		
Manipulated		
Mean		
Miserable		
Misunderstood		
Moody		
Mysterious		
Natural		
Nervous		
Nice		
Open-minded		
Panicky		
Pleasant		
Private		
Proud		
Quiet		
Reasonable		
Relaxed		
Relieved		
Repulsed		

NOTES

Sexuality

Suggestions	Add	Something like this
Right		
Rigid		
Rough		
Safe		
Satisfied		
Scared		
Selfish		
Sensible		
Sensual		
Serious		
Sexual		
Shy		
Sick		
Sincere		
Sorry		
Spasticity		
Special		
Strong		
Stubborn		
Tender		
Tense		
Terrible		
Trusting		
Ugly		
Understanding		
Uneasy		
Upset		
Uptight		
Withdrawn		

NOTES

Suggestions	Add	Something like this
Sexual Activity		
Accept		
Allow		
Anal sex		
Arousal		
Assault		
Behind		
Caress		
Choose		
Come		
Cuddle		
Cum		
Decide		
Dream		
Dress		
Ejaculate/ejaculation		
Emotion		
Emotional abuse		
Enter		
Erection		
Erotic/erotica		
Excited		
Experiment		
Exploration		
Facing		
Fantasy/fantasize		
Force		
Grunt		

TIPS

You may want to use slang words for many of the vocabulary items in this section.

Suggestions	Add	Something like this
Hug		
Hurt		
Intercourse		
Lick		
Lie down		
Lubricant		
Make noise		
Masturbation/masturbate		
Moan		
Moist		
Oral sex		
Orgasm		
Penetrate		
Physical abuse		
Pornography		
Position		
Protection		
Put on		
Push		
Rape		
Remove		
Rub		
Sensation		
Sex		
Sex toys		
Sexual abuse		
Sexual drive		
Side by side		

TIPS

Sexual Abuse

The risk of sexual assault for women with disabilities is up to five times higher than for women without disabilities, and the risk increases with the severity of disability (Sobsey, 1994).

Abusers are often people in positions of trust and authority (Sobsey & Varnhagen, 1988).

People who cannot communicate cannot prevent or report assault, cannot gain access to the justice system, and are unable to receive counseling. It is essential that AAC users have access to the vocabulary they need in order to communicate about and prevent sexual abuse.

Suggestions	Add	Something like this
Stroke		
Swollen		
Top		
Touch		
Under		
Undress		
Unwanted sexual activity/ advances		
Value		
Verbal abuse		
Vibrator		
Wait		
Wash		
Wet		
Wet dream		
With consent		
Without consent		
Other:		

TIPS

The *Being Sexual* series of books by Hinsburger and Ludwig (1993) provides important sexuality education for young adults. The clear text and illustrations are particularly helpful for people with developmental disabilities; literacy, learning, or communication problems; or anyone who uses Blissymbols.

Ludwig's (1995) *After You Tell* guides readers through the experiences that may occur after someone discloses that he or she has been sexually abused. Blissymbol translation appears throughout the text.

These books are published by:

Sex Information and Education Council of Canada (SIECCAN)
850 Coxwell Avenue
East York, Ontario
M4C 5R1
Canada

17

Clarifying Your Message

This chapter addresses two problems that result in a conversation partner not understanding a message conveyed by a person who uses augmentative and alternative communication (AAC). A problem may occur when you do not have the words—either on your display or in your device—that you need to communicate your message. This chapter includes some phrases that you might want to use when asking your partner to guess what you mean.

Another problem may occur when the correct words are available, but for some reason your partner cannot figure out what you mean. You may have accidentally jumbled your words, or your partner may have forgotten words that you have already communicated. Perhaps the partner assumes incorrectly that he or she knows what you are communicating. Some of the following phrases may help you give feedback to your partner and tell him or her what he or she can do to understand your message.

Suggestions	Add	Something like this
When You Do Not Have the Word You Need		
I'm having trouble spelling the word I want. I'll give you a clue. Try to guess what I mean.		
I don't have the word (or picture or symbol) I need. I'll give you some clues. Try to guess what I mean.		
I think it starts with the letter		
I'm not sure how to spell it, but I'll try.		
It's a (thing, place, person, animal, feeling, action).		
It's like		
It's about		
It's used for		
It's the opposite of		
It sounds like		
It starts with		
It has something to do with		
It's part of		
You would see it		
Other:		

TIPS

Steps to Take When You Do Not Have the Word You Need

1. Tell your partner immediately. This lets him or her know that he or she is going to have to work with you to figure it out.
2. When giving clues, start with the most general clue before getting specific. For example, if you want to communicate about a specific make of car and you do not have the words, tell your partner
   - I don't have the word I need. I'll give you some clues.
   - It's a ______ car or vehicle.
     It is made in ______.
   - Please guess.
3. Practice giving clues. A great way of doing this is playing games of 20 Questions (but not during a conversation).

Suggestions	Add	Something like this
Helping a Partner Guess		
Please guess.		
Please don't guess until I'm finished. I'll let you know when to start.		
You're close.		
You're way off		
Go back. You were closer before.		
Keep trying.		
You've nearly got it.		
That's it. Well done!		
Thanks for trying.		
I know it's frustrating.		
This is important.		
This isn't important. Let's forget it!		
Other:		

TIPS

Helping a Partner Guess

Take control. Do not just let him or her guess randomly.

Tell your partner that you want him or her to guess or that you do not want him or her to guess.

If you want your partner to guess,

1. Give good clues
2. Give clear "yes" and "no" responses to your partner's suggestions
3. Tell your partner when he or she is close to—or far from—the correct answer
4. Congratulate your partner when he or she gets the answer

Suggestions	Add	Something like this
When Your Message Is Misinterpreted		
That's not what I meant.		
Let's start again.		
Please write down the words as I communicate them.		
Please say what I have communicated so far. I'll let you know when you get to the bit that's wrong.		
Please repeat every word I select.		
Tell me what you understand so far.		
Please try to put my words into a sentence.		
I forget where I stopped. Please say what I have communicated so far.		
Thanks for trying, but let's drop the subject.		
It's important.		
It's not important.		
Let's try that again.		
Let's forget it.		
Ask me again later.		
I'll try again later.		
Can we come back to this later?		
I know this is hard for us.		
Please ask ______. He (or she) knows what I am talking about.		

TIPS

When Your Message Is Misinterpreted

When your message is misinterpreted, consider the following:

- Is it because your partner does not know how you communicate? If so, ask your partner to read your introduction card for instructions.
- Is it because your partner cannot remember the words you have communicated? If so, ask your partner to write the words down.
- Is it because your partner interrupts and guesses? If so, tell your partner to wait until you have finished communicating.
- Is it because your words are jumbled? If so, ask your partner to try to put your words into a sentence.

Suggestions	Add	Something like this
Please ask me yes/no questions.		
Let's go to ______. I can show you something that will help you guess.		
Other:		

TIPS

What to Do When All Fails

- Get someone else to try to guess.
- Ask your partner to ask you questions.
- Decide how important your message is and whether you want to proceed or drop the subject.
- Look up the word/picture in a dictionary or use object clues if appropriate.

18

Death and Bereavement

When a loved one passes away, people may have feelings of shock, numbness, and disbelief. They may feel overwhelmed and panicked and may experience strong physical and emotional reactions. Some people deal with their grief by communicating about the event, the person who passed away, and their feelings. Some people need to repeat these stories as a means of dealing with their grief.

Augmentative and alternative communication (AAC) users need to be able to express themselves in these situations. It is important to have words for these occasions and to have opportunities to communicate about events, feelings, and reactions. This chapter provides suggested vocabulary to help you express yourself. Bereavement support services may be available in your community or through a local church organization. A social worker may also be able to assist you.

Death and Bereavement

Suggestions	Add	Something like this
Death		
Death/dead		
Die/dying		
Passed away/deceased		
Life/living/lived		
Did not survive		
Sick/ill/illness/serious condition		
Suffer/suffered		
Wake		
Visitation		
Viewing		
Funeral/service/memorial		
Funeral home		
Church/chapel		
Grave		
Graveyard/cemetery		
Scatter area		
Tombstone/memorial		
Burial/cremation		
Flowers		
Donations		
Obituary/death notice		
Hearse		
Casket (open/closed)		
Urn		
In memory		
Body/remains/ashes		

TIPS

Although there is a close link between religious beliefs and how one deals with death and bereavement, religious words have not been included in this chapter. It is suggested that you incorporate your own religious and spiritual vocabulary.

Suggestions	Add	Something like this
Grieving		
Mourn/grieve		
Worry		
Sad		
Cry		
Tears		
Shock		
Scared		
Lonely		
Afraid		
Depressed		
Angry		
Out of control		
Withdrawn		
Apathy/lack of interest		
Tight chest		
Palpitations		
Shortness of breath		
Diarrhea/constipation		
Lack of energy/weak		
Restless		
Change in appetite		
Change in sleep pattern/ insomnia		
Numb		
Empty		
Indifferent		
I need to think about		
I can't stop thinking about		

TIPS

Two years after John's father died, John continued to suffer extreme grief and loss to the point that he could think of little else and saw no meaning in his own life.

John could not spell and, therefore, relied on other people to give him the vocabulary he needed in pictures. Everyone was afraid of upsetting John, so nobody gave him words to communicate about his father's death.

Recognizing that he needed to communicate about this event and his feelings, John selected the words he needed and participated in choosing what he wanted to tell partners about his father's death. A display (in the form of a pictorial sequence of events) was made to illustrate what happened to his father, the funeral, and words for John's feelings.

Six months later, John is getting on with his life. He rarely communicates about this event but chooses instead to tell stories about his father's life and personality. John's mother thinks that this healthy change is due to the fact that John has "talked it all out of his system" and that he now knows that he can communicate about it at any time.

Suggestions	Add	Something like this
Confusion		
It doesn't seem real.		
I'd like to be alone.		
I'd like some company.		
I'd rather not talk about it now.		
Thanks for listening.		
Thanks for being there.		
Poor concentration		
Forgetful		
Denial		
Disbelief		
Daydream about the past		
Blame		
Other:		

NOTES

Suggestions	Add	Something like this
Hearing About a Death		
I'm sorry to hear		
Please accept my condolences.		
I was shocked to hear		
Did _______ suffer?		
Was it expected?		
Please accept my sympathy.		
I'd like to send flowers.		
I'd like to send a donation.		
I'd like to send a card.		
What is the address?		
What happened?		
When did it happen?		
Where did it happen?		
Who was there?		
How is the family?		
What are the funeral arrangements?		
Other:		

NOTES

19

Legal Vocabulary

As augmentative and alternative communication (AAC) users become more empowered to determine the life they want to live, they are seeking information about their rights and how they can exercise them in their daily lives. In situations in which their rights have been violated, AAC users are beginning to gain access to the legal system. As with other conversational contexts, AAC users need the words to communicate and learn about their role in court.

The vocabulary in this chapter is based on Farrar's (1996) book *End the Silence: Preventing the Sexual Assault of Women with Communication Disabilities: Developing a Community Response* and Prem-Stein and Clemis's (1995) communication tool *Legalpix–A Pictorial Journey Through British Columbia's Criminal Justice System.*

Suggestions	Add	Something like this
General Terms and Phrases		
Abuse		
Acquit		
Accused		
Adjournment		
Arrest		
Assault		
Audiotape		
Bail		
Broken law		
Breaking and entering		
Charge		
Complainant		
Consent/no consent		
Corroboration		
Court		
Crime		
Crown counsel		
Defense counsel		
Defense lawyer		
Deliberation		
Evidence		
Found guilty/not guilty		
Fingerprint		
Give evidence		
Government		
Guilty		
Impaired driving		

TIPS

Legalpix–A Pictorial Journey Through British Columbia's Criminal Justice System (Prem-Stein & Clemis, 1995) is a set of pictures that illustrates words describing concepts, people, places, and processes associated with the justice system in British Columbia, Canada. Also included is an educational guide with specific lessons, a guide for using *Legalpix* as a communication tool, and a dictionary of 98 pictures representing concepts and components of the justice system.

For more information, contact:

Kindale Developmental Association
Post Office Box 94
Armstrong, British Columbia
VOE 1B0
Canada
(614) 546-3005

Suggestions	Add	Something like this
Inquiry		
Investigate/investigation		
Interview room		
Jail		
Judge		
Justice system		
Jury		
Lay charges		
Law		
Narcotics abuse		
Perjury		
Photograph		
Police		
Police car		
Police station		
Plaintiff		
Plea		
Plead guilty/not guilty		
Preliminary hearing		
Probation		
Probation officer		
Prosecution		
Reasonable doubt		
Reasonable/unreasonable force		
Robbery		
Search		
Sentence		
Shoplifting		

TIPS

Jim charged his attendant with sexual assault. He made his statement to the police using his communication display. Prior to proceeding with the arrest, the police needed Jim to demonstrate a sound understanding of the consequences of a court trial. A picture communication display containing legal vocabulary and an educational program were developed. Jim learned about the process, and he later showed that he understood what lay ahead and wanted to proceed with the trial.

Legal Vocabulary

Suggestions	Add	Something like this
Statement		
Subpoena		
Suspect		
Summons		
Tell the truth		
Testimony		
Testify under oath		
Theft		
Trial		
Vandalism		
Verdict		
Videotape		
Voluntary statement		
Warning		
Willful damage		
Withdrawal		
Written statement		
Witness		
Other:		

NOTES

General Terms and Phrases

References and Vocabulary Resources

Balandin, S., & Iacono, T. (1998). A few well-chosen words. *Augmentative and Alternative Communication, 14*(3), 147–161.

Balandin, S., & Iacono, T. (1999). Crews, wusses, and whoppas: Core and fringe vocabularies of Australian meal-break conversations in the workplace. *Augmentative and Alternative Communication, 15*(2), 95–109.

Beukelman, D.R., McGinnis, J., & Morrow, D. (1991). Vocabulary selection in augmentative and alternative communication. *Augmentative and Alternative Communication, 7*(3), 171–185.

Beukelman, D.R., & Yorkston, K. (1982). Communication interaction of adult communication augmentation system use. *Topics in Language Disorders, 2*(2), 39–54.

Beukelman, D.R., Yorkston, K., & Poblete, M. (1984). Analysis of communication samples produced by adult communication aid users. *Journal of Speech and Hearing Disorders, 49,* 360–367.

Collier, B. (1999). Learning to communicate with attendants. *Communicating Together, 16*(1), 15–16.

Collier, B. (2000). *Communicating matters: A training guide for personal attendants working with consumers who have enhanced communication needs* [Videotape and manual]. Baltimore: Paul H. Brookes Publishing Co.

Elder, P.S. (1994). Vocabulary selection for vocational training activities with augmented speakers who are moderately/severely developmentally delayed. In *The Pittsburgh Employment Conference, 2,* 56–60. Pittsburgh, PA: SHOUT Press.

Elder, P., & Goossens', C. (1996). *Communication overlays for engineering training environments books 1, 2, 3, & 4.* Solana Beach, CA: Mayer-Johnson Co.

Elder, P., & Goossens', C. (1996). *Engineering training environments for interactive, augmentative communication: Strategies for adolescents and adults who are moderately/severely developmentally delayed.* Solana Beach, CA: Mayer-Johnson Co.

Farrar, P. (1996). *End the silence: Preventing the sexual assault of women with communication disabilities: Developing a community response.* Calgary, Canada: Technical Resource Centre.

Fried-Oken, M., Creech, R., & Baker, B. (1994). *Pragmatic issues for natural and augmented speakers in the public venue.* Presented at the 1994 Biennial Conference of the International Society for Augmentative and Alternative Communication, Maastricht, The Netherlands.

Fried-Oken, M., & Stuart, S. (1992). A few selected words about word selection: Vocabulary issues in AAC. In D.J. Gardner-Bonneau (Ed.), *The second ISAAC Research Symposium in AAC* (pp. 68–78). Philadelphia: International Society for Augmentative and Alternative Communication (ISAAC).

Hingsburger, D., & Ludwig, S. (Series Eds.). (1993). *Being sexual.* East York, Canada: Sex Information and Education Council of Canada (SIECCAN).

King, J., Spoeneman, T., Stuart, S., & Beukelman, D. (1995). Vocabulary selection for augmentative communication systems: A comparison of three techniques. *American Journal of Speech-Language Pathology, 2*(2), 19–30.

Krezman, C., & Williams, M. (1991). Tips and techniques for talking on the telephone (interpreter issues). *Augmentative Communication News, 4*(4), 6–7.

Light, J., & Binger, C. (1998). *Building communicative competence with individuals who use augmentative and alternative communication.* Baltimore: Paul H. Brookes Publishing Co.

Lindsey, P., & Millin, N. (1998). Sexuality. *Communicating Together, 16*(1), 2–3.

Ludwig, S., (1995). *After you tell.* East York, Canada: Sex Information and Education Council of Canada (SIECCAN).

Myers, C., Gibbons, C., Fried-Oken, M., & Bersani, H.A. (1996). Self-advocacy core vocabulary for augmented speakers with intellectual impairments. In *Proceedings of the Seventh Biennial Conference of the International Society for Augmentative and Alternative Communication* (pp. 543–544). Vancouver, British Columbia, Canada.

Newell, A. (1992). Social communication: Chattering, nattering and cheek. *Communication Outlook, 14*(1), 6–8.

Nosek, P. (1989). *Busting loose to independence through personal attendant services: Everything you need to know about finding, hiring, maintaining—and if necessary firing—your personal care attendant (pca)* [Audiotape set]. Houston, TX: Division of Education, The Institute for Rehabilitation and Research (TIRR).

Prem-Stein, J., & Clemis, M. (1995). *Legalpix–A pictorial journey through British Columbia's criminal justice system.* Armstrong, Canada: Kindale Developmental Association.

Roeher Institute. (1997). *Out of harm's way: A safety kit for people with disabilities who feel unsafe and want to do something about it.* North York, Canada: The Roeher Institute, York University.

Sobsey, D. (1994). *Violence and abuse in the lives of people with disabilities: The end of silent acceptance?* Baltimore: Paul H. Brookes Publishing Co.

Sobsey, D., & Varnhagen, C. (1988). *Sexual abuse and exploitation of people with disabilities: Final report.* Ottawa, Canada: Health and Welfare Canada.

Stuart, S. (1988). Vocabulary selection-augmentative communication. *South Dakota State Speech-Language Hearing Journal, 31,* 17–19.

Stuart, S., Vanderhoof-Bilyeu, D., & Beukelman, D. (1994). Differences in topic reference of elderly men and women. *Journal of Medical Speech-Language Pathology, 2*(2), 89–104.

Williams, M. (1994). How do you say *hamburger? Alternatively Speaking, 1*(1), 4–5.

Yorkston, K.M., Smith, K., & Beukelman, D. (1990). Extended communication samples of augmented communicators 1: A comparison of individualized versus standard single-word vocabularies. *Journal of Speech and Hearing Disorders, 55,* 217–224.

Appendix A

Adding to Your Personal Vocabulary by Category

This manual contains a compilation of words and phrases that augmentative and alternative communication (AAC) users may find useful in specific situations. However, much of what we communicate relates to our personal interests and work and the people in our daily lives. The following list of categories can be used as a guide for selecting the personal vocabulary you may need in your AAC system. Add other categories that are relevant to you.

People

Include the names of important family members, friends, attendants, employers, educators, service providers, neighbors, and so forth.

Places

Include places where you currently go or went in the past; specific names of stores; cities and countries where you, family, or friends live; and so on.

Significant past events

You might want to include stories about vacations, weddings, births, and other memorable events.

Favorite sayings, slang, jokes, and curse words

Most people reflect their personality and culture through their communication. AAC users can do this as well by giving input to those who program or add words to their AAC systems. AAC users should be able to communicate what they want in their own way.

Favorite foods and drinks

Hobbies or interests

Include not just a list of your hobbies, but also vocabulary you need to communicate about your hobbies.

Religious worship/events

To participate in spiritual activities, you might want to have prayers and hymns programmed into your device or put on your display.

Health/disability issues

Consider your specific service instructions for attendants, doctors, and service providers.

Work

You will need personalized vocabulary to communicate at work.

Appendix B

General Resources

Alternatively Speaking
Augmentative Communication
1 Surf Way
Suite 237
Monterey, CA 93940
sarahblack@aol.com
http://www.augcominc.com

The Aphasia Centre–North York
53 The Links Road
North York, Ontario
M2P 1T7
Canada

Augmentative Communication News
Augmentative Communication
1 Surf Way
Suite 237
Monterey, CA 93940
sarahblack@aol.com
http://www.augcominc.com

Blissymbolics Communication International
630 Lawrence Avenue West
Suite 104
Toronto, Ontario
M6L 1C5
Canada
http://home.istar.ce

Communicating Together
3-304 Stone Road West
Suite 215
Guelph, Ontario
N1G 4W4
Canada
(519) 766-1757
www.ahs.uwo.ca/orcn/assoc/comtog

Communication Aid Manufacturers Association (CAMA)
Post Office Box 1039
Evanston, IL 60204-1039
cama@northshore.net

International Society for
Augmentative and Alternative Communication (ISAAC)
49 The Donway West
Suite 308
Toronto, Ontario
M3C 3M9
Canada
(416) 385-0351
www.isaac-online.org

Kindale Developmental Association
Post Office Box 94
Armstrong, British Columbia
V0E 1B0
Canada
(614) 546-3005

Pittsburgh Employment Conference (PEC)
SHOUT
Post Office Box 9666
Pittsburgh, PA 15226
(800) 668-4202 or (412) 885-0943
SHOUT@sgi.net

Roeher Institute
York University
Kinsmen Building
4700 Keele Street
North York, Ontario
M3J 1P3
Canada
http://indie.ca/roeher/index.html

Sex Information and Education Council of Canada (SIECCAN)
850 Coxwell Avenue
East York, Ontario
M4C 5R1
Canada

Technical Resource Centre
200, 1201-5 Street Southwest
Calgary, Alberta
T2R 0Y6
Canada
(403) 262-9445